Fictional Technique
in France, 1802-1927

Fictional Technique in *France* 1802-1927

AN INTRODUCTION

JOHN PORTER HOUSTON

LOUISIANA STATE UNIVERSITY PRESS

BATON ROUGE

PQ
651
.H6

ISBN 0–8071–0041–2

Library of Congress Catalog Card Number 72–181568

Copyright © 1972 by Louisiana State University Press

Manufactured in the United States of America

Printed by Vail-Ballou Press, Inc., Binghamton, New York

For Natalie

Introduction

THIS BOOK IS AIMED primarily at an audience of students; its scope is introductory. There have been many interesting works on fictional technique published in English and in our century: Henry James's contact with Flaubert's circle would seem to be at the origin of them. They tend, however, to discuss English and American fiction, with only an occasional glance at such European writers as Stendhal and Dostoievsky. Among the more recent and best-known of them, Wayne Booth's *The Rhetoric of Fiction* (Chicago, 1961) shows exemplary modesty in eschewing anything more than an occasional and unpretentious observation on French, German, and Russian novels.

In France the most striking essays on fictional technique have tended to be highly polemic, perhaps since they are often the work of novelists themselves, eager to establish some firm theoretical ground for rejecting their predecessors' conceptions of the novel. Gide, Proust, Sartre, and Robbe-Grillet have been especially vocal. The polemical spirit, of course, rises up in special circumstances, is generally unwilling to accept a plurality of fictional methods, and has, in any case, no intention of presenting a dispassionate account of the novel's evolution. There is nothing in French which quite resembles the American academic studies on the subject. The study of individual writers and their techniques has fared better in both French and English: Victor Brombert's studies of Stendhal and Flaubert or Maurice Bardèche's books on Balzac and Stendhal have treated certain questions in a manner that it is not exaggerated to call definitive, and Martin Turnell's *The Novel in France* (New York, 1951) and *The Art of French Fiction* (New York, 1959) examine the major writers, though not primarily with regard to technique. These books have furthermore been complemented by Harry Levin's *The Gates of Horn: A Study of Five French Realists* (New York, 1963), a massive examination of the realist author's relation to his times, which allows us to forego discussing certain questions about the novelist's vision and his place in society. We shall deal with most of the same major authors as Professor Levin, but we shall confine ourselves to the narrower matter of how the author creates his illusion. This will, furthermore, entail the consideration of some lesser novels: in so inventive a literary period as nineteenth-century France there are abundant minor masterpieces, and if we try to reconstruct the evolution of literature at that time, we find that, say, *Mademoiselle de Maupin* was read, admired, and imitated by writers whose gifts we tend to rank above those of Gautier.[1] On the other hand, there are certain lesser novelists who enjoy minor reputations, but who did not, I feel, contribute especially to technical innovation. Maupassant is one, and when other such

[1] See Enid Starkie's various remarks in *From Gautier to Eliot: The Influence of France on English Literature* (London, 1960).

omissions occur, they are due not merely to personal prejudice against this or that novel, but to what I think to be the irrelevance of the work or author to the guiding theme of our inquiry. Novels can be interesting for a great number of reasons, but technique alone concerns us here.

The method of this study is relatively traditional. Point of view and various narrative devices used to convey it are examined, as well as plot structure and symbolic elements in overall composition. Fictional time, chapter and part structure, and stylistic peculiarities of the narrating voice receive perhaps more than the usual emphasis. My aim is to avoid any too dogmatic or systematic approach to the novel in favor of investigating the particular area of technique in which a writer has been most inventive.

The dates 1802–1927 may seem obscure, but they mark the publication of *René*, the earliest novel we shall treat in any detail, and the year in which *Thérèse Desqueyroux* and the last volume of Proust's novel appeared.

The text of this book is intended to be readable for those who know little or no French; only an occasional quotation has been left in French, and only in cases where the style is such as to make it impossible to render it adequately in English. The footnotes are conceived of as a highly selective bibliography of the best in studies on individual writers.

Contents

Fictional Technique
in France, 1802-1927

1

Stendhal and Pseudorealism

THE CONVENTIONS of the eighteenth-century and nineteenth-century novel are strikingly different although they stem from a common concern: to make of the novel a serious form of literature. In the eighteenth century this was accomplished by presenting the novel as a document, as a piece of writing allegedly taken from reality.[1] Thus the epistolary novel was a favorite genre as was the first-person narrative. Framing devices were important for adding to the documentary illusion; prefaces tell how the letters were found or when the editor heard and wrote down someone's life story. These prefaces tend also to insist on the value of the work as a moral example, be it positive or negative, with the result that even licentious fiction could be judged socially useful. Some of these prefaces are obviously parodies, such as the one to *Adolphe*, the last great novel in the eighteenth-century tradition, in which the editor sug-

[1] Techniques are discussed in Vivienne Mylne, *The Eighteenth-Century French Novel: Techniques of Illusion* (Manchester, 1965); attitudes toward the novel in Georges May, *Le Dilemme du roman au dix-huitième siècle: Etude sur les rapports du roman et de la critique 1715-1761* (New Haven, 1963).

3

gests that no one will be edified because people always think they are superior to characters in fiction. While the "editor" of *Adolphe* never even tells us the exact nationality or habitual language of his main character or, much less, when the events took place, a nineteenth-century realist like Balzac, on the other hand, records the baron de Nucingen's Alsatian accent in French and identifies the street on which a house is situated, as well as the precise year of the action. The nineteenth-century novelists did not feel that their work was primarily a moral example, but rather that it was a form of historical, sociological, and psychological knowledge. Thus the characters are frankly fictional, but representative of a type of person in the context of a specific society at a specific time. There is a paradox underlying nineteenth-century realism: it is both specific and general, fictive and true. However, it is this paradox which freed the novelist from the somewhat stiff conventions of the eighteenth century and allowed the growth of far more varied techniques of fiction than had previously existed. While the theory of realism is logically untenable, the results of it are artistically justified.

II

The paradox of realism is nowhere more evident than in the work of Stendhal. The world of *La Chartreuse de Parme* has been described as a "devaluation of reality" [2] whereas Auerbach said of *Le Rouge et le Noir:* "The characters, attitudes, and relationships of the dramatis personae, then, are very closely connected with

[2] Judd D. Hubert, "The Devaluation of Reality in the *Chartreuse de Parme*" in *Stendhal: A Collection of Critical Essays*, ed. Victor Brombert (Englewood Cliffs, N.J., 1962).

contemporary historical circumstances; contemporary political and social conditions are woven into the action in a manner more detailed and more real than had been exhibited in any earlier novel, and indeed in any works of literary art except those expressly purporting to be politico-satirical tracts."[3] The problem seems to lie in the fact that, while details of clothing and custom, manner and mode of life are abundant in Stendhal, the characteristic tone of his novels makes one doubt that he had a genuine concern for documentary seriousness. Auerbach's mention of politico-satirical tracts seems to me a more useful guide to the thematics of *Le Rouge* than any notion of realism, especially since ambivalence and ambiguity between author and character, author and reader prevail, with effects that are continually surprising. On the surface we are especially conscious of the author's interventions; here is the scene in which the "liberal" jailor, Valenod, has the prisoners silenced in order that his formal luncheon not be interrupted:

> With his glass in his hand, Julien remarked to M. Valenod, "They're not singing that vulgar song anymore."
> "By God, I should think not!" M. Valenod answered triumphantly. "I've had the rabble reduced to silence."
> These words were too much for Julien—he had the manners but not as yet the mentality of his present position. In spite of all of his frequent practice of hypocrisy, he felt a big tear stealing down his cheek. . . .
> Fortunately no one remarked his ill-bred emotion. The inspector of taxes had struck up a royalist song. During the rollicking refrain, sung by everyone in chorus, Julien's conscience was telling him: There you see the filthy riches you'll acquire—and you'll not have them save on such conditions and in company like this! . . .
> I must say the weakness Julien shows in this soliloquy gives me a poor opinion of him. He would be a worthy

[3] Erich Auerbach, *Mimesis* (New York, 1957), 403.

colleague of those yellow-gloved conspirators, who aspire to change all the ways and habits of a great country yet shirk having to reproach themselves with responsibility for the slightest drop of blood.

Julien's sentimental overreaction is only a subtler form of hypocrisy than the one he has been cultivating and criticizing: the prisoners' misfortune provides simply an opportunity for Julien to demonstrate to himself what a sensitive creature he is, without his being moved to better the lot of the prisoners. He is, in short, making rhetorical phrases for himself, which is the ultimate form of self-deception. The author's intervention about yellow-gloved conspirators (yellow gloves were very fashionable) is necessary to prevent the reader from misconstruing Julien's superior sensibility. These interventions often take the peculiar form of a contrary-to-fact conditional sentence: "The following morning Mme de Rênal was alone with him for a moment in the drawing-room.

'Haven't you any other name except Julien?' she asked him.

Our hero did not know what to reply to so flattering a question. Such a circumstance had not been anticipated in his plan. Had it not been for his stupidity in making one, Julien's quick intelligence would have served him well—surprise would only have made his observations all the livelier." This way of suggesting opposite possibilities accounts for some of the curiously animating effect of Stendhal's intrusions into the narrative: it underscores the character's choice in his actions, as well as his emotional and intellectual limitations.[4]

We might best discuss the texture of *Le Rouge et le*

[4] For detailed analysis of Stendhal's themes and "interventionism" see Victor Brombert, *Stendhal: Fiction and the Themes of Freedom* (New York, 1968).

Noir by recourse to the notion of a palimpsest: one sees all sorts of obvious words and meanings on the surface; beneath, however, are several different layers. The top one is a kind of pseudorealism, which is actually a parody of political and social life, with the author making a running commentary on the absurdity of society and its institutions; next comes a series of amusing classical heroicomic conventions; and buried down below is a mythic pattern of the hero's irruption into life, his battle, his death, and his return to the forces of nature. The problems in interpreting Stendhal seem all too often to have been created by inability to see several coexistent but intermittent levels of meaning. With Stendhal one tends more to run the risk of oversimplifying than that of overinterpretation.

Le Rouge et le Noir is one of the most allusive novels in French literature; far from being merely realistic and documentary it feeds continuously on the great tradition of European literature, as may be seen by the abundance of epigraphs, many of them doubtless invented, and especially those taken from Byron's *Don Juan*. (Wayne Booth has observed that an epigraph is a remarkable form of authorial intervention.) Although epigraphs were popular among the French romantics, few used them as much as Stendhal and few with such effect. The whole Mme Rênal-Julien episode is commented on by lines from Byron's poem. While Stendhal does not, in fact, quote the following, he obviously had in mind passages like this:

> Juan she saw, and, as a pretty child,
> Caress'd him often—such a thing might be
> Quite innocently done, and harmless styled,
> When she had twenty years, and thirteen he;
> But I am not so sure I should have smiled

> When he was sixteen, Julia twenty-three;
> These few short years make wondrous alterations,
> Particularly amongst sun-burnt nations.
> . . . .
> Yet Julia's very coldness still was kind,
>   And tremulously gentle her small hand
> Withdrew itself from his, but left behind
>   A little pressure, thrilling, and so bland
> And slight, so very slight, that to the mind
>   'Twas but a doubt; but ne'er magician's wand
> Wrought change with all Armida's fairy art
> Like what this light touch left on Juan's heart.

> (Canto I, LXIX, LXXI)

By his use of epigraphs Stendhal maintains a whole surreptitious point of view about Mme de Rênal: she is feminine, a bit stupid, hardly immoral, but terribly confused, and surely erotically frustrated in all her innocence. Byron puts it with a more faun-like smile; Stendhal contents himself with indirect allusions which bring forth recollections of Byron's bawdier passages.

The first part of *Le Rouge* is constructed according to themes which derive from heroic literature: the duty to oneself (seducing Mme de Rênal), vanity, playing a role, energy, pride. The novelty of Stendhal's treatment of all this is his contrasting the heroic, aristocratic ethic, which he admires, despite its anachronism, with a newer one in which the instinct for happiness, love, reverie, and sincerity are even more admirable. Comedy results from the discrepancy between heroic duty to oneself and the desire for happiness. There is, therefore, a superposition of heroic themes over an essential criticism of them, and only through elaborate authorial intervention can this be conveyed. Stendhal is actually making a synthesis of the conventional psychologies of literature from the neoclassical period to his own time. The stylistic forms this takes are frequently imitations of seventeenth-century drama: a long monologue will consist of alternating between two paths of action, such as we find a good deal of in Corneille. Stendhal was not concerned with finding a more novelistic way of rendering these altercations with self. One of the great charms, actually, of Stendhal is that he mingles genres and conventions: theater is about as thoroughly combined with narrative as it could be. From a very early point in the novel we are aware that the characters are playing "scenes," which they have rehearsed. Theater is equated with insincerity, since it is not spontaneous and therefore cannot bring happiness: Julien's liaison with Mathilde will, in this respect, repeat that with Mme de Rênal, but the theatrical atmosphere will be even more pronounced.

There is another dimension, however, to *Le Rouge* —that lowest layer of the palimpsest we have mentioned. The episodes of the grotto and the news clipping found in the church show that Stendhal is constructing an essentially poetic novel: these passages go beyond the bounds of ordinary realism, for Stendhal has a predilection for placing thematic augurs and hints, much in the fashion of epic. "The greatest distinction for a man is to be condemned to death," Mathilde says casually in Part II, and this exemplifies the *thematic* unity we associate with poetry rather than the *causality* of fiction.

Another poetic dimension of the novel comes from Stendhal's use of archetypes, for each of the main characters of *Le Rouge* has a mythic or historic antecedent. In Mme de Rênal's case, it is the châtelaine de Vergy, whose lover's heart was fed to her in the old Provençal tale. Mathilde de la Mole adores her sixteenth-century ancestor, Boniface de la Mole, and at the end of the novel will become symbolically identified with his mis-

tress. As for Julien, the only episode in the opening
chapters of Part II that is not social parody is his visit
to La Malmaison, which is a pilgrimage, that is, a *sacred*
undertaking. Napoleon is Julien's patron saint, and his
holy text the *Mémorial de Sainte-Hélène*. These archetypes, while giving some psychological plausibility to
the behavior of, say, Julien and Mathilde, principally
add affective richness and sweep to the narrative. They
also—and this is very characteristic of novels in which
stable thematic motifs count for more than the causal
chain of incidents—are more prominent than so essential
a narrative element as time: one can easily construct a
chronology for *Le Rouge* (or *La Chartreuse*), but in
reading the novels we are not vividly aware of season
and lapse of time; Stendhal followed a perfectly justifi-
able time scheme in writing the novel, but he did not
make of it the structural element that later novelists did.

While Part II of *Le Rouge* abounds in the social comedy Stendhal was so expert at (whose counterpart in
Part I is the seminary episode, an amusing *étude de
moeurs*), it also contains the thematic center of the
novel: the chapters where the conventions of theater so
strongly dominate the narrative that we actually feel
the relations between Mathilde and Julien to be a somewhat ironic re-creation of scenes from seventeenth-
century drama. There are allusions to Corneille: "au
milieu de tant de périls, il me reste MOI," Mathilde says,
misquoting Medea, while Julien contends, with a "gas-
con" accent, that "Il y va de l'honur." However, since
in the elaborate dialectic of genres and tones which
Stendhal has established, comedy, heroism, and theater
of any kind are the enemies of sincerity and happiness,
Julien and Mathilde are trapped in a convention which
does not correspond to their emotions; they create

heroicomic patterns unsuited to the reality of seduction and thus hardly know what to say to each other when they find themselves in bed together. A "sincere" reseduction is then necessary, carrying out the pattern set in the Julien-Mme de Rênal episode: one might say that the ethic of Rousseau triumphs over that of Corneille. The plot structure of *Le Rouge* is not continuous, in terms of causality, from beginning to end. Just before and just after Mathilde's seduction, the book reaches a still point with little further promise of plot development. This still point is rather characteristic of longer works of fiction in the nineteenth century: it serves to break up the action into well-defined large parts—a dramatic analogy suggests itself—which are, however, bound together by common thematic material. The anonymous letters (whose function is symmetrical to the ones in Part I, just as the seminary episode has as its pendant the secret diplomatic journey) are obviously a crude device by any reasonable and realist conception of the novel of manners. Happily Stendhal is *not* writing a novel of manners, which means that this bit of melodrama can be accepted simply as a device, a means toward an end, like the prophecies and premonitions in Corneille's plays. In one of the really amazing foreshortenings in French fiction, Julien determines to leave Paris, gets to Verrières, and shoots Mme de Rênal, all in one page.

What follows indicates best the genre and meaning of *Le Rouge et le Noir*. Stendhal's amusing comments about the Faubourg Saint-Germain in 1829 are no more than amusing; they do not reveal the imagination of a great writer in the way the concluding chapters of the novel do. Julien *sleeps*, the word is repeated over and over; the rest of mankind—including Mathilde—

becomes foreign. More important, he recalls all the
poetry he has studied (he, who has never had any normal education), and his last words in his farewell letter
to Mathilde are Iago's "From this time forth I never will
speak word" (quoted in English!). In other words, the
range of literary allusion with which Stendhal comments
on his story has moved from mock epic (*Don Juan*)
through Cornelian tragicomedy (the *Cid* echoes) to
tragic poetry. The discreet color of Stendhal's own
style is reinforced by these references, which help, furthermore, to effect a shift from the heroicomic psychological vocabulary of the Verrières and Paris episodes to
the dreamy, detached mood of the prison chapters.
Here Stendhal is making a bold change of convention:
the military and aristocratic ethic which has hitherto
governed Julien vanishes as his end draws near, and he
becomes a new kind of hero. It is as if we were shifting
from drama to romance, from a psychologically
grounded convention to a mythic one, and specifically
to a cyclic pattern: when Mathilde buries his head in
the grotto, from which he saw himself setting out to
conquer Paris, she is fulfilling a legendary pattern, repeating the actions of the *amante* of her ancestor, Boniface de la Mole.

The ending of *Le Rouge et le Noir* is an important
key to Stendhal's imagination and to the interpretation
of his two most famous novels. The fact that *Le Rouge*
builds up to so antirealist a conclusion should make one
suspicious of any kind of reading of Stendhal which fails
to take account of why Julien is made, at the end, into
an anachronistic kind of hero: one superior in spirit to
other men, guided by a distinct force of fate, and
mysterious in his origins (Julien's alleged father surely
could not have produced him). Julien is obviously a

changeling, sent into the world to upset it like the Per-
cevals and the swan-knights of legend, and who returns
finally into the natural order whence he came. One
kind of critic has always been willing to ignore the details of the conclusion or to call it unsatisfactory, since
sociological interpretations will not work. It is only, I
think, by recognizing a profound tendency toward
heroic romance that we can do justice to Stendhal's art.[5]
The tendency toward romance and mythic situations
which we have seen at work in *Le Rouge* reaches its
fullest expression in *La Chartreuse de Parme*. Like a
heroic poem rather than a realist novel, it has, not a
causally tight plot, but an episodic—and richly thematic
—account of Fabrizio del Dongo's life. The motif of
pageant and theater becomes clearly associated with
nobility of spirit; spatial and geographic symbolism is
prominent; but the themes most in evidence are those
connected with the hero's life and destiny in traditional
romance. Aside from the allusions to Tasso and Ariosto
and to Fabrizio's numerous devoted servants and ani-
mals, we find the narrative of a fabulous (in the sense of
"story-like") childhood utterly involved, not with men,
but with nature and with the supernatural as well (in
the figure of the Chiron-like abbé Blanès), with omens
and portents such as the eagle's flight which dispatches
Fabrizio to Waterloo, and with many other marks of
the hero which we shall have occasion to notice.

From the standpoint of literary sources as well, we
find a contrast with *Le Rouge et le Noir*: the latter had
behind it, at least partially, the story of the criminal
Berthet, a rather sordid episode which might reasonably

[5] For the best-known and most useful discussion of heroic romance, see Northrup Frye, *Anatomy of Criticism* (Princeton, 1957),
33–36.

be considered as belonging to class warfare; *La Char-treuse*, on the other hand, was inspired by sixteenth-century tales such as the *Origine della grandezza della famiglia Farnese* and Benvenuto Cellini's account of his escape from the Castel Sant'Angelo.[6] At first, the political theme in *La Chartreuse* might seem to have some realist-historical meaning, were it not for the fact that Stendhal invented the politics of Parma (they appear to have been inspired by those of the next-door duchy of Modena). However, Stendhal was, as it has been said, an atheist in politics, and as a novelist his commitment is only to certain characters and never to a political ideology. He kept his own clashes with parties and factions as absent from his novel as possible. Conservatism and liberalism are mocked to the same degree; only a vague allegiance to the Napoleonic era betrays emotions which for Stendhal must have been beyond ideology and more identified with his youth than with a specific ruler.

La Chartreuse also differs from *Le Rouge* in that it is a story of happiness, freedom, all-but-fulfilled love, and self-denial, in which so many of the decisions affecting moral and sentimental life are made directly and freely by the characters of the novel that it is not astonishing that existentialist readings of the work have had some currency. However, as we shall see, the predetermination of the hero's life, as revealed through astrology, and the fateful vow taken by Clelia assume a very different conception of the world than that of Sartre and his disciples.

The comic-opera flourishes of the opening of *La Chartreuse* (the French army's upsetting traditional

---

[6] Such matters are investigated in Maurice Bardèche, *Stendhal romancier* (Paris, 1947).

mores) as well as the theatrical court intrigues of the later parts have been called a devaluation of reality, but I prefer to see them somewhat more positively as an attempt frankly to banish realist conventions, despite the relative contemporaneity of the events. Balancing the political comedy is the story of Fabrizio's childhood. He is evidently an illegitimate child (Stendhal constantly suggests more than he says in *La Chartreuse*); furthermore he is a natural believer—if unorthodox—even a mystic. He knows principally nature—exemplified by his tree, that is, his tree of life—and he is initiated into its secrets by his tutor, the abbé Blanès, who teaches him augury. All this section has its roots in mythology, notwithstanding the brilliant episodic account of life in Milan at the court of Prince Eugene. This combination of the romantic-worldly and mythical romance is the essence of the peculiar and enchanting tone of *La Chartreuse de Parme*.

Fabrizio's adolescence must necessarily include a trial, which is a traditional hurdle in growing up to be a hero. Interestingly enough, Stendhal chooses a completely realistic convention for this episode, which is Fabrizio's journey to take part in the Battle of Waterloo. The speech is colloquial ("va te faire f. . . . ." and "et moi-itou"); girls suddenly become interested in him during his convalescence; and, through being robbed and thwarted, Fabrizio passes from being an inexperienced ninny into a mature young man. Yet, despite the superficial realist coloring, other events occur which belong more to a novel of predestination and fatality: Fabrizio glimpses his real, French father at the battle; and when he is being surreptitiously brought by his aunt and mother from Lombardy (Austrian and therefore anti-Napoleonic) into the freer state of Piedmont, he meets Clelia Conti, "who would be a charming prison companion."

The border incidents upon Fabrizio's return to Italy may seem at first merely to add a bit of gratuitous suspense to the novel, but actually they bring out a basic theme: frontiers, passports, police lists, and prisons are designed to limit the very *idea* of freedom in the individual. Geography is the most important way, in *La Chartreuse*, of rendering this sense of liberty and confinement. Place—the Italian lakes, the states of the Po Valley, the Austrian-held or independent duchies —assumes the kind of importance that time patterns have in most fiction, and we must be constantly aware of geopolitical implications: it is important, for example, to remember that Bologna belonged to the Papal states, that Piedmont was a monarchy free from foreign intervention, and so forth.

At this point the major plot quietly vanishes: the next few years of the narrative are devoted to La Sanseverina and Mosca's success in Parma society and local intrigues. Fabrizio meanwhile is studying theology in Naples and learns—a capital theme in the novel—that he is incapable of love. In a submerged fashion this discovery guides his decisions in much that follows. Fabrizio has, of course, affairs, much like the affection for a favorite horse, as he remarks somewhere, and after his arrival in Parma, where his aunt has planned a great career for him, Mosca sends him away in order to avoid gossip about his unduly close attachment to an actress. This temporary dismissal of Fabrizio from Parma is one of those episodes which seems only vaguely motivated, a bit lengthy, and generally loose in regard to the larger structure of the novel. However, it is a fine example of Stendhal's use of slight narrative pretexts to introduce an essential part of his thematic design. Fabrizio goes to meet his mother on the Piedmontese side of Lake Maggiore. This passage represents a return and farewell to childhood and youth, which is further emphasized by Fabrizio's clandestine entry into Lombardy and his native places around Lake Como. This is also, in another sense, a journey of self-discovery: the night he spends in the company of the abbé Blanès and the prediction of prison he receives from the astrologer clearly determine his destiny. Fabrizio is now the mature hero in possession, like Achilles, of the knowledge of his fatal weakness, of the *moira* that separates him from the demigods.

Technically it is important to note that this episode contains another description of Lake Como and its landscape, which have already been depicted. Stendhal tends, to a remarkable degree, to avoid physical description, unlike his contemporaries, whose great exemplar was Chateaubriand. This tendency is so strong that we must consider any tableau as extremely vivid and quite symbolic in import. The language Stendhal uses in portraying Gina's going back to Lake Como (Chapter 2) as well as Fabrizio's delight in returning there (Chapter 9) is, however, less sensuous than emotive: the lake is "sublime," "nothing so beautiful can be seen in the world,"—in short the lake incarnates "happiness." Stendhal rarely uses any concrete terms; he adheres to the late neoclassical vocabulary of description that we find in Rousseau and other eighteenth-century writers for whom the affective qualities of language are more important than visual preciseness. But although the words are the insipid poetic ones of Stendhal's youth, they stand out by contrast with the rest of the narrative, even as an old-fashioned poem of Lamartine's could, in the right context, seem striking. To measure the significance

other Alpine peaks which stretch from Nice in the direction of Mount Cenis and Turin." This passage is a complete departure from Stendhal's normal descriptive style; the panoramic effect, the proper nouns, and the notations of quality of light almost sound like Chateaubriand. Stendhal uses this sort of style only to indicate something very important: Fabrizio's prison will paradoxically bring him freedom, the freedom which comes through love, and so the first thing he sees is an immense view, which symbolizes liberty. This landscape is, of course, a mental one and completely stylized: from a jet plane one cannot see from Nice to Treviso, much less if one were atop a tower in Parma; in short, the purely imaginative character of the description underscores its thematic value. Imprisonment for Fabrizio will constitute a realization of himself.

Balancing Fabrizio's discovery that his imprisonment brings happiness—that the abbé Blanès' prediction works out differently from what he had thought—is Clelia's vow, at the time her father is drugged, never to look on Fabrizio again. Thus Fabrizio's fondness for his prison is cancelled out by the superstitious interdiction which Clelia imposes on herself. The odd mixture of astrological readings, portents, and vows gives a characteristic coloring of the supernatural to the novel, which occasionally becomes especially vivid as in the passage relating Fabrizio's escape from the Citadel. (Stendhal suddenly lets Fabrizio narrate, in retrospect and from a limited point of view, the seemingly impossible way he slipped through the guards.)

The second sojourn at Belgirate, which Fabrizio makes after his escape from Parma, brings up again the notion of thematic structure as opposed to plot development: Lake Maggiore, while rich in reminiscences, no longer means anything to him, just as La Sanseverina has ceased to occupy a major place in his emotive life. His experience of height, both physical and moral, has been transferred from the Italian lakes to the tower on the grim plain of Parma, the lakes belong to the duchess, the lowland to Clelia and his fate.

At this point we become more and more aware of the bifurcation which is taking place in the plot: it has by now sorted itself out into a Sanseverina-Mosca line and a Fabrizio-Clelia one. The narrative switches from one couple to the other, but now they are seldom found engaged in working toward the same ends. Initially the duchess dominates these chapters (21 through 27) and for good reasons: she is the one who settles, as best she can, the situation in Parma, and is made to do so in an astonishingly elliptic manner. First of all, there is the understated, if not enigmatic, passage in which she orders Ferrante Palla to have the prince poisoned. Far clearer is the accompanying order to have Parma flooded and Sacca illuminated with fountains of wine. In other words, Stendhal, as so often, is suppressing somewhat our awareness of an ugly action and superimposing on it a grand and noble, not to say theatrical, gesture. Morally the duchess is probably justified, but it is principally by the style in which she commits tyrannicide that one is won over to her side.

The second situation in which Stendhal and La Sanseverina conspire to hide facts from the lazy reader occurs during the brilliant year of entertainment when the duchess again dominates Parmesan society. It is the burning of secret state papers involving espionage which the duchess proposes: toward this end she has the new prince read aloud the La Fontaine fable about "Le Jardinier et son seigneur," which concludes with an ad-

monition to "little princes," who risk losing everything
if they call in a major power during wars. Stendhal is
here playing a very subtle game with the reader: since
no great power is threatening Parma, the duchess' advice
seems at first gratuitous and whimsical, but with careful
rereading, one realizes that La Sanseverina is referring,
in a most guarded fashion, to the fact, alluded to much
earlier in the novel, that Mosca has foresightedly hidden
in Austrian Lombardy state documents which could, if
known to the Hapsburg authorities, provoke an immediate annexation of Parma by force. The reader cannot
know how aware the new prince or his mother is of this
potential tool for blackmail: Stendhal preserves a delicate
ambiguity. Of course, this ambiguity then leads to
another plot development, when the new prince, jealous
of the duchess' powers, forces her to submit to him. This
art of half highlighting an incident so as to leave psychological and moral questions forever suspended in mystery
characterizes the duchess' last days in Parma, an episode
which also benefits from Stendhal's peculiar sort of
abridgment of events: the prince's insistence on sexual
conquest of the duchess is treated with the greatest rapid-
ity and deftness of touch, just as was her order to assas-
sinate his father; there is an unfailing sense of taste in
La Chartreuse, whether the subject be murder, perjury,
or prostitution.

When the duchess has left Parma, Fabrizio and Clelia
occupy center stage, and now the shape of the whole novel
becomes clearer: it might be described as a court comedy
of great brilliance framed, at the beginning and end, by
a heroic romance. Of course, the heroic romance in the
persons of Fabrizio and Clelia intrudes frequently on the
comedy in which the duchess and Mosca are acting, but
that Stendhal chose to begin and end his novel with

Fabrizio points up the heroic-romantic substructure of the work.

The later pages of *La Chartreuse* have been criticized, especially the concluding ones, for tending to tell, rather than show, that is, to narrate rather than dramatize. (That Stendhal's publisher wanted him to limit the number of pages is neither here nor there: great writers make do with arbitrary constraints.) However, the technique of this section is quite essential to the larger design: Stendhal is attempting an effect of distancing as the novelistic illusion draws to its end. Various little details suggest that Clelia and Fabrizio are growing older—their age is now more that of Antony and Cleopatra than of Romeo and Juliet. Narrative time is being telescoped. Fabrizio disappears more and more into a nebula of mysticism, hypocrisy, and amorous fervor, as his sermons become famous erotico-religious experiences in the fashionable world. It is significant that Stendhal does not attempt to give us a sample of these texts.

Myth becomes more obtrusive as the *liaison* between Fabrizio and Clelia commences: she, because of her early vow, can meet him only in darkness, a variation on the Psyche and Eros legend, in which the existence of an interdiction prevents complete fulfillment of the relation. But the meetings in the darkened orangery lead to the birth of a son, and a further twist of fate, that fate which, as earlier, is full of ambiguities. Sandrino's feigned death turns out to be a real one; Clelia's ill-kept vow becomes, for her and Fabrizio, the force of destiny. Retreats in towers conclude the latter's existence, for the circle of his life is complete: he has returned to the heights—be they Alps or towers—whence he came. All this, of course, is narrated, not shown dramatically, since the world of *La Chartreuse* is beginning to vanish into fiction

and myth: the revels now are ended, and these our actors
melted into air.

III

Balzac wrote a lengthy review of *La Chartreuse de
Parme*, in which he noted sagaciously how few contemporaries would have the intelligence to understand the
book and pointed out the brilliance of certain episodes.
At the same time, however, Balzac suggests that the
structure of the book leaves much to be desired, and
here, in this conflict of conceptions between two great
novelists, we can learn a great deal about the art and the
aspirations of both. To put it succinctly, what Balzac
liked above all was the realism of the court intrigue centering on La Sanseverina and Mosca. He was obviously so
taken with the parodies and other comic devices that he
failed completely to see that Mosca's and the duchess'
behavior depends on something more than the absurd and
sinister court of Parma. On the other hand, the account
of Fabrizio's childhood and the last section dealing with
the liaison between Fabrizio and Clelia simply left Balzac
cold. He was incapable of seeing anything but dull writing and plotlessness in the parts of the novel dominated
by heroic romance. Balzac, in short, read the novel with
no intuition of Stendhal's conventions; instead, he tried
to make it conform to his own notions of realism, which
portrayed events with chronological exactitude and
strong implications of causality. Balzac's esthetic is much
closer to the more ordinary twentieth-century conception of the novel: he liked a tight plot line informed by
strict temporal patterns. In contrast Stendhal's seemingly
casual fictional technique stresses theme above plot
structure, poetic conceptions above ordinary verisimili-

tude. Stendhal is much closer to the great earlier narratives of western literature such as the *Iliad* or medieval romances, in which we do not find a beginning-to-end enchainment of action, but rather a plausible, if episodic, sequence of events: the fact that in the course of the nineteenth century readers became more and more accustomed to a more modern logic of plot should not obscure the fact that far more of the great narratives in earlier western literature were conceived of in the same terms as Stendhal's, rather than in those of Balzac, Flaubert, or Zola.

2

Balzac and La Comédie humaine

"No one begins, to my sense, to handle the time-element and produce the time effect with the authority of Balzac in his amplest sweeps."[1] Henry James's praise might better apply to Proust, whose work he could not have known, but it suggests one of the most novelistic aspects of Balzac's work, and one which Stendhal, for all his greatness, did not have. It is possible, as editors have done, to construct a chronology for Stendhal's novels, but the reader never really feels the passage of time brought home to him as he does in Balzac's mature work. At his best, Balzac had that broad command of imaginary time and space which is the privilege of great novelists. However, he did not attain this skill without years of work, much of which was of little merit. To say nothing of the gothic novels of the 1820s, which he did not even sign, Balzac's first realist literary productions strike one as examples of *costumbrismo*, as it was called at that time in Spain: vignettes of contemporary life and types, which do not have plot so much as anec-

---

[1] Henry James, *The House of Fiction: Essays on the Novel*, ed. Leon Edel (London, 1957), 82.

dote, fictional time so much as the simple chronology of an oral account. The road from anecdote or melodrama to the realist novel, much less to a cycle of novels, was a long one. There are, however, a few guideposts. With *La Duchesse de Langeais* (1833–34), containing its allusion to *La Femme abandonnée* (1832), and parts of *La Fille aux yeux d'or* (1833), we already have elements of that society which will constitute the nucleus of *La Comédie humaine*, at least insofar as it is Parisian. There is Mme de Beauséant, the grandest of the great ladies, and de Marsay, the fashionable and immoral illegitimate son of the aristocracy. The levels of society are being sketched out, and key types exemplified. What we do not find in these works, however, is a satisfactory mode of narration. *La Duchesse de Langeais* seems, almost pointlessly at times, to avoid chronology in favor of a melodramatic but hardly effective or clear sequence of events. *La Fille aux yeux d'or*, on the other hand, fails to integrate the opening discourse on Paris with the lurid anecdote which follows. In short, James's time effect is lacking, and this may well come from the shortness of the narratives, the limited number of characters, and Balzac's inexperience at weaving a balanced plot.[2]

Le Père Goriot (1834–35) does, however, contain the amplest of "sweeps," both in its varied depiction of Parisian life and, more important, in its temporal structure. The opening sequence, despite some regrettable details of style, consists of a subtle, progressive exposition which can hardly be separated from the beginnings of the narrative itself. The gradually increasing focus on November 1819, the mingling of accounts of Rastignac's origins with his activities on a specific evening, and the

[2] Balzac's early work is examined in detail in Maurice Bardèche, *Balzac romancier* (Paris, 1947).

many fragmentary details about various characters lead us into a morning following the brief night scenes, and the tableau of the Pension Vauquer, the point of departure of the novel, is completed by the dinner at which the *externes* are present. At least several plot lines are already in evidence, and while the first pages suggest the naïvely schematic beginning of an old movie, the subsequent succession of incidents is quite elaborately interwoven. One interesting thing in particular slowly emerges: Balzac presents a number of facts through the eyes of Rastignac; he is gradually settling us into the latter's point of view. Despite the fact that we associate Balzac with very free intervention on the author's part, he is quite capable of establishing and maintaining with reasonable consistency various kinds of limited vision.

With Rastignac's consciousness fixed as the dominant one in the novel, the first long continuous episode begins, that in which he successively visits Mme de Restaud and Mme de Beauséant. Here we see, for the first time, the time pattern that will prevail in this and other of the finest Balzac novels. Although Balzac used chapter divisions (which were eliminated by one of his publishers and are only to be found in scholarly modern editions), they are less important structurally than the breaking-up of the plot into days: the lengthy day is the unit he favors in shaping a narrative. The day may contain contrastive or unrelated events; its function is to give an effect of forward propulsion, of increasing intensity in the main character's experience. The reason for this is that Balzac's more memorable characters "say to themselves" (*se disent*) very little in comparison with Stendhal's. Their will to power of whatever sort is not tempered by introspection; they are bent on collision courses with one another, and they express themselves principally through action and interaction. Although intellectual and moral values may touch them on occasion, their driving urge to possess or control necessarily implies a kind of plot where confrontations abound. To order such elaborate episodic material, Balzac found that clearly delineated, sometimes almost interminable days would best structure the characters' progress and its impact upon the reader. One or two examples from *Goriot* come to mind especially: the day when Rastignac receives money from home, has his first interview with Vautrin, dines with Mme de Beauséant, goes to the theater, and meets Delphine; or the one when Vautrin is arrested, Victorine becomes an heiress, Rastignac is led off to his *garçonnière*, and the Pension Vauquer is emptied. A complementary device to the use of the long day is the continual repetition of "the next day" suggesting that events never lose their headlong rush forward.

The texture of Balzac's novels has been so often criticized that it is hardly worth repeating here all the objections raised. It is certainly true that the middle-class fustian which came into being with the Revolution and Empire left its mark on Balzac's style: the urge toward pseudoelegant periphrases is especially evident. However, Balzac had a more complex sense of language than he is usually given credit for. Here and there, as when Rastignac notices that he is talking to Mme de Beauséant in "hairdresser's language," it is perfectly clear that the affectation is not Balzac's but his character's. At the same time, Balzac can speak as bombastically in his own voice: when Poiret is described, at the point where he and Mlle Michonneau are contacted by the police, Balzac gives us half a page of analogies between climates as they vary according to latitude, and salaries as they vary among the bureaucratic ranks. (A happier example of his imposing a narrator's tone is the heroicomic passage in *Illusions perdues* about the Flicoteaux restaurant.) It seems to be especially in bridging passages and descriptions that Balzac's style undergoes unfortunate elaboration as if he were afraid of the reader's interest flagging. To be sure, the simple fact of elaboration has nothing to do with its quality: Proust could have handled brilliantly the latitude-salary analogy I have just mentioned. Proust, furthermore, is the most perceptive analyst of Balzac's style: [3] he remarked that Balzac "had all the elements of a true style but never fused them properly." His metaphors are those of a great raconteur, not a stylist. Proust saw in the texture of Balzac's fiction a peculiar defect—of which Dickens and Dostoievsky might also be accused—that of satisfying the reader's urgent need to hear more of the story, while withholding from him a feeling of real finish. There is a hasty jumble of better and worse in such a style, and one suspects that the worst parts occur when the novelist has not imaginatively realized his scene or character but is relying on handy clichés or a convivial manner that does not withstand the test of print.

Proust goes on to point out that there is certainly some unfortunate telling rather than showing in Balzac. This one has to agree with, but I doubt that many critics have really noticed how much is left implicit and unstated in *La Comédie humaine*. I think it is more valuable, rather than discussing the linguistic details of so bewilderingly eclectic a style, to point out how the author's avoidance of local comment or interventions functions remarkably well, and less intermittently than one might think, in a novel like *Goriot*. We tend to remember certain appallingly shrill authorial comments such as calling Goriot the

[3] See the references in *Contre Sainte-Beuve* (Paris, 1954).

"Christ of Fatherhood," but these lapses—which can be matched in other French romantic writers—must not make us forget how much Balzac does not say, how much his dialogue presented without commentary damns his characters, and how great is the lack of harmony between their speech and their actions. An example: Balzac observes early, apropos of Rastignac, that the young "cannot see themselves in the mirror of conscience." Rather later, when Rastignac is shown into the elegant flat Goriot and Delphine have set up for him, he exclaims, "I'll be worthy of all this!" Delphine's comment: "What you've just said is beautiful." When you analyze the words "all this," it becomes clear that they denote little more than a rather coarse bargain, which could even seem to border on prostitution, were it not that both parties to the agreement have ambitions which far transcend the erotic. The latter is merely a pretext, and the reader has no difficulty in so guessing, since the discrepancy between word and deed touches on the ludicrous; Delphine says, "If I want more than ever to move in the Faubourg Saint-Germain, it's because you're there." Of course, the pretty sentiments are to vanish in subsequent novels, and, enriched by Delphine's husband's aid, Rastignac will marry their daughter.

Balzac does some other subtle things with dialogue presented without commentary in briefly sketched settings. This is, of course, an adaptation of theatrical methods, such as the overheard conversation (difficult to render in old-fashioned narratives with any smoothness); a broad piece of comedy occurs near the end of the novel when Rastignac, overhearing from the next room Mme de Restaud plead for money from her father, unexpectedly walks in and offers it to her. She then denounces Delphine's vulgarity in permitting her lover to spy on them, but grabs the bankdraft (no comment) and leaves. A moment later she returns in a fit of forgiveness since, as Rastignac observes, she needs a signature on the draft. All this is pure theater: Balzac's fictional technique, like Stendhal's, reveals his early interest in drama.

However, the real originality of *Le Père Goriot* lies in the adjustment of an intricate but lucid plot structure to a varied, well-defined group of characters. To begin with, the novel is one of initiation, the first of many subsequent ones in the French realist tradition. Rastignac is learning the ways of the Parisian aristocracy, and this point of view permits even quite complex patterns in society to appear not as gratuitous complications of plot, but as necessary details of the whole we are trying to grasp. There are almost countless parallels and antitheses among the characters and events of the novel. Eugène has the option between Victorine, a marriage proposed by Vautrin, and Delphine, Goriot's choice for him as mistress; the two older men are contrasting father figures. Delphine and her sister represent the rival claims of wealth and aristocracy; Vautrin and Mme de Beauséant share the same view of society, and Vautrin's ring of crooks is more honest than the world of the supposedly law-abiding. Delphine enters the noble Faubourg as Mme de Beauséant is leaving it, and so forth.

So powerfully constructed a novel tended to draw other narratives into its orbit: it serves as the inspiring and determining force in Balzac's subsequent production, as well as in the reshaping of much which precedes it. An especially striking example of this refashioning process is the story *Gobseck*, originally published in 1830 as a *scène de la vie privée*, and revised in 1836 as part of *La Comédie humaine*. In the original form of *Gobseck*, there was a Mme de Restaud, who mishandled family diamonds, and a Jew, brilliant and legalistic as Shylock, who took advantage of her foolishness. Balzac kept the name Restaud, made it an important one in *Goriot* and redid *Gobseck* in 1836 as a satellite narrative of *Le Père Goriot*, and one in which the Restaud family drama occupies an important place. In formal terms, it might be best to speak of works like *Gobseck* as chapters or interludes in the central, Parisian area of *La Comédie humaine*. Structurally *Gobseck* resembles an episode in Proust: a few privileged people are got together over dinner (the framing device), and one of them tells the story. (It is worth noting that the narrator, the lawyer Derville, is one of the characters whom Henry James described as *ficelles* and who, while seldom the real subject of a narrative, constantly reappear and serve to reveal, in a neutral fashion, facts about major *personae*.) Keeping in mind the analogy with *A la recherche du temps perdu*, we can discover from this a good deal about Balzac's imagination: *La Comédie humaine* is composed of a very few great narratives which we can structurally consider novels according to the criterion of plot development; at the same time, Balzac wrote a fair number of shorter pieces, some of which could hardly be called short stories in the formal sense, since there is little "showing" or dramatization of the story: these are "chapters" in the larger scheme of *La Comédie humaine*. There are one or two curious examples beside *Gobseck* of Balzac's refitting of early work to match his later plan: the two very *grandes dames* of *Goriot*, Mme de Beauséant and Mme de Langeais, had already been accounted for in their later lives a year or two before *Goriot* was written, in *La Femme abandonnée* and in *La Duchesse de Langeais*.

Goriot not only absorbed but also generated certain

short narratives. *La Maison Nucingen* (1838) is especially interesting in this respect since it cannot be called a dramatized story and is meaningless outside the framework of *Goriot* and later novels. Technically it shows Balzac at his most inventive: an anonymous member of the world of *La Comédie humaine*, who knows both the Faubourg Saint-Germain and the world of journalists, is dining at an elegant restaurant. In the next private dining room he hears Balzac characters discussing Nucingen's fortune and its origins, as well as Rastignac's rise in the world. The technique is odd, probably unsuccessful, but quite original: there is a first person who, though nameless, is very much a part of Balzac's fashionable world, and the story is constructed almost exclusively out of dialogue. *La Maison Nucingen* enriches our sense of the characters without being, in itself, overly interesting, for the account of financial maneuvering is both complete and dull. The episode is hypertrophic, an odd interlude, but no more an independent piece of fiction than any detached chapter might be: we should see parts of *La Comédie humaine* as an assembly of subworks, whose value depends totally on another context. A variation on the same pattern can be found in *Autre étude de femme* (1842), where again an anonymous member of Balzac's fictional world dines with, rather than overhears, almost every person in fashionable society under the July Monarchy. These people tell stories: the dinner party is again a framing device. What is especially interesting here is that for the last tale, which the famous Doctor Bianchon tells, Balzac adapts a brief story, *La Grande Bretèche*, which he had written some years before. Once the conception of *La Comédie* was established, he seems to have had a need to draw into it as much of his earlier work as possible.

La Maison Nucingen and *Autre étude de femme* have in common another important effect: they deal with characters who were young in the early 1820s and who, by now (around 1835), are well settled into middle age. They share memories of events and persons and thereby give to *La Comédie humaine* a strong feeling of the passage of time, of generations succeeding one another. They induce in the reader a similar sense of both recollection and curiosity about details of certain characters' lives which are being divulged for the first time, even though the events themselves belong to the distant past.

In the late 1830s Balzac's imagination was at its most fertile. He wrote, beside a number of satellite narratives, the first two parts of his longest and greatest novel, *Illusions perdues*, which as an initiatory novel goes far beyond *Le Père Goriot*. Lucien is destined to learn not only provincial and Parisian aristocratic mores, but also the ways of journalism and political intrigue. George Lukács [4] definitely stated the thematic content of the work: taking his customary aristocratic point of view (which, as Henry James once pointed out, can be more a device of fictional technique than a political conviction) Balzac shows that from paper making to newspaper publishing, from novel writing to book selling, his era had been corrupted by the most irresponsible forms of early capitalism and debasement of taste. Lukács completely justifies Balzac's disquisitions such as that on the manufacture of paper; what I want to do here is to show how great a formal achievement *Illusions perdues* is, quite aside from its ethical and historical significance.

The exposition of *Illusions perdues* occupies some seventy pages, which is long, but not overly long for

[4] See George Lukács, *Studies in European Realism* (London, 1950), 47–64.

Balzac; almost half of *Ursule Mirouët*, one of his less successful works, consists of exposition, while his works which begin directly with a scene often have clumsy, involved plots with which a present-day reader may well lose patience. The important fact about the exposition of *Illusions perdues* is its use of various kinds of fictional time. All time in fiction is, of course, illusional, but it may be handled with greater or lesser degrees of skill or elasticity. Henry James's comment on Balzac's time effects are especially relevant here. The Romance languages have a greater choice of past tenses than the Germanic ones, but Balzac's subtlety in the handling of time goes beyond the mere advantage of having an imperfect and a *passé simple* to distinguish between. In the beginning of *Illusions* we can observe several different narrative tempi and time planes. There is the distant past, in which the origins of persons and institutions are accounted for, the more immediate past dealing with recent events in Lucien's life, and the descriptive passages in the imperfect tense, which renders habitual actions or states. These are all mingled for variety. Portraits, bits of scenes, anecdotes, summary narration, and authorial interventions provide a constant change of narrative pace, while temporal loopings back—a favorite technique of Balzac's—continually enrich and diversify the exposition. There is nothing mechanical or dry about the accounts of previous events; they constantly change in perspective and, by their intermittent references to a future fixed date when the plot will begin (Lucien and David's discussion of Chénier in 1821), have a dynamic forward thrust.

Balzac's onomastics, always a very important part of his imagination, are at their very best in *Illusions:* the change from Lucien Chardon (a real peasant appelation:

thistle) to the fancy sounding M. de Rubempré is delightful, while the name of Louise de Nègrepelisse (*black fur*, with an old, heraldic ring) designates her as the child of the noble and crest-stricken. Finally, there is Châtelet, Lucien's rival for Mme de Bargeton's favors (Balzac subtly designates her as Louise de Nègrepelisse or Mme de Bargeton according to her role as *amante* or lady). Châtelet's name also changes with his role. The form Monsieur du Châtelet (the name of a prison familiar to readers of *Manon Lescaut*) is used largely in Part II, when, in Paris, he occupies *le haut du pavé*; in Angoulême, where Empire nobility is essentially a scandal, he is usually just plain Châtelet. Balzac's witty variation in usage does not depend solely upon sections of the novel, however; the texture of the sentence and paragraph also determines it; noble onomastics could not be more delicately exploited.

As for the question of point of view, the anonymous narrator, that is, the implied author, has some clearly visible traits of his own; while in one sense he is the more or less omniscient narrator associated with fiction before Flaubert, he is also certain other things: a well-connected Parisian, who can only be amused at provincial manners, a judge of the particular value of certain aspects of nobility, and a social critic of conservative but not reactionary cast. Above all, he looks downward and with detachment on his characters. Theme and point of view change utterly in Part II, without, however, an inartistic break in technique between the parts. The reason is that Lucien is not a little *poétiau* in Angoulême, but a young man struggling, like Rastignac before him, to make something of himself in the capital. We now see everything from his point of view, from that of a poor student making an encyclopedic study of the means of subsistence open to a literary man in Paris. Louise, who, "poetized, tragicized, angelized, and colossified," recedes into the background of tedious old climbers and culture vultures, while Lucien's plight becomes the most terribly poignant one in Balzac: Lucien turns into a pathetic, self-deluding figure as he ceases to be the over-inflated genius of Angoulême.

The first months of Lucien's stay in Paris are narrated in a slow-paced fashion; this change of tempo, after the tense duel and flight from Angoulême, is characteristic of Balzac, who had a fine sense of contrasting narrative movement. Then comes the long day, the device we have discussed in regard to *Goriot:* it lasts about 100 pages out of some 750 (which shows its significance) and in it, Lucien, and the reader, are initiated into the world of journalism, book selling, and the theater. This is perhaps Balzac's finest example of giving the reader everything at once, in one unit of time and in tight sequence.

One of the most ambiguous parts of this section concerns Lucien's writings. His sonnets were, of course, taken from Gautier and others; the poems quoted in Part I are by Balzac himself (circa 1827); his theater review is presumably from Balzac's hand. Taken as a whole, these pieces represent typical, if minor, genres of the period, and very mediocre, if not downright bad, examples of them. One of the most delicate problems in interpretation comes up here: by any modern reading, Lucien is a dreadful writer, his verse, borrowed or not, belonging to the weaker romantic strains, his drama review insipidly cute in an elephantine way. Even the salon idiots in Angoulême realize that his verse (Balzac's in this case) is puerile. What in the world did Balzac mean by having his "genius" be such a fool? The answer comes, I think, with Lucien's sinking into the cesspool of journalism. The whole story, as Lukács sees it, is one of corruption, but there is also something else, which a Marxist critic perhaps could not understand: Lucien is essentially *no good* as a writer—his prose is trashy, his verse derivative; he belongs in journalism. But Balzac refrains from commenting on all this, which is an exceptionally fine piece of stategy: he successfully divorces his own weaknesses from those of Lucien. We could never conceive of Lucien's writing *Illusions perdues*.

The time pattern in the later section of Part II of *Illusions perdues* consists first of a relatively vague chronology, which contrasts both with the long day which precedes and the "fatal week" which follows, and in which time thickens as Lucien's downfall becomes imminent. Just before that week, however, we encounter a sudden and rather surprising change of point of view. We know that Lucien, incapable of resisting flattery, has been won over to the Royalist party. Now, as we enter the thoughtstream of the vengeful Mme d'Espard, we realize that Lucien will be a victim of his illusions, which gives the true measure of the title of the work and the psychological basis of the plot. Lucien's triumphs, like becoming the lover of Mme de Bargeton or of Coralie, or his specious success in journalism always turn against him: no sooner has he achieved something than it loses its value for him as well as for others.

To return to the problems of narrative technique, however, it is important to note that a switch in point of view from the main character to a conspiratorial group already occurs in *Goriot*: the scene in which Poiret and Mlle Michonneau meet the detective in the Jardin des Plantes. The reader, who has been lulled by the main character's point of view, is startled at the altered per-

spective. In *Illusions* the change of point of view comes
when we learn, through her, that Mme d'Espard has been
plotting against Lucien. This kind of shifting between
antithetical viewpoints seems at times a trifle clumsy
in that it interrupts the narrative tone; yet Flaubert used
it abundantly in *Madame Bovary*, where its ironic possibilities are thoroughly exploited. Balzac's use of it may
be more haphazard, but one cannot imagine Flaubert's
practice without the mediation and example of Balzac.

Again toward the end of Part II, as Coralie is dying and
Lucien is obliged to write drinking songs to earn money,
the time pattern of the narrative relaxes into notations
of month, rather than day or week. This change is by
no means unimportant in its effect upon the reader:
after a series of disastrous days and events, the narrative
pace slows to an almost somnolent state, which corresponds to Lucien's increasing feelings of despair, failure,
and social rejection.

The third part of *Illusions perdues* is perhaps the
most striking example in Balzac of the *retour en arrière*
or looping back. The antecedents of this device are to
be found in epic: Homer, Virgil, and Milton make use
of the looping back after a plot begun *in medias res*,
but their use of it involves the presence of a speaker,
like Odysseus or Aeneas, who is obliged to tell his tale
for one practical reason or another. By looping back I
do not mean this kind of narration on the part of a
character, nor do I mean the traditional sort of paragraph, or two, which introduces a new character—
"Mme X. had always had a penchant for parakeets and
Christmas trees." What I designate by looping back is
an impersonal narration which begins with the clearly
marked statement of a time point which has already
been passed. This new kind of *retour en arrière*, of

which I have been unable to find examples in French literature before Balzac, tends to have an ironic relation to the story with which it contemporaneously exists. In *Illusions* the ironic parallel is between Lucien's downfall in the world of journalism and David Séchard's in manufacturing the material, newsprint, which journalism presupposes. The two narratives are neatly synchronized by the letters which Lucien or his friends have sent to the Séchards.

Loopings back are often constructed so that the second narrative goes beyond the temporal limits of the first: such is the case in the middle of Part III of *Illusions*, where Lucien's return to Angoulême marks the end of the plot dimensions of Part II. The short concluding section of the novel, which leads into *Splendeurs et Misères des courtisanes*, contains one of the finest scenes in Balzac: the encounter between Carlos Herrera and Lucien, who is about to commit suicide, or who at least thinks he will, is the most dramatic example of the recurrence of characters, which, *dixit* Proust, is Balzac's greatest fictional invention. All here depends on details of style. The dialogue is especially effective, although the authorial commentary is worthy of Proust, who carefully imitated it in the second part of *A l'ombre des jeunes filles en fleurs*, where the narrator first sees Charlus. "This traveler seemed like a hunter who has found a lengthily and hopelessly sought after prey." The intense drama of the scene, which can be felt only in the context of *Goriot*, comes when Herrera-Vautrin repeats to Lucien, almost word for word, the theory of ethics he had revealed to Rastignac: "Have you ever thought about the deep friendship between two men . . ." and he again refers to Otway's *Venice Preserved*. Lucien now acquires a new diction to match the self-consciously unctuous one of the supposed Spanish priest. He becomes pseudopoetic and flowery, as when, to refuse a cigar, he says: "Je suis trop près du terme de ma course pour me donner le plaisir de fumer." Herrera-Vautrin is all oiliness and affectation, while Lucien becomes vaguer as a personality. Lucien is making that pact with the devil which d'Arthez had earlier predicted and is becoming the shadowy tool—Vautrin's *créature* —that he will be in *Splendeurs et Misères;* the scene has an eerie sort of fade-out effect as far as Lucien as a personality is concerned.

It is therefore not surprising that in the sequel Balzac appears to change genres: *Illusions perdues* has, besides its sociological dimension, a carefully worked out psychological one in which variation follows variation on Lucien's fundamental swaying between generosity and egotism. Once Vautrin enters his life, there are no more decisions for Lucien to make, and *Splendeurs et Misères* is conceived of as a superior tale of intrigue centering on Vautrin's struggle with the secret police, but ranging in its ramifications from duchesses' salons to the convicts' prison courtyard. Disguises are everywhere; psychological motivation is cut to a bare conventional minimum to make way for an immensely involved yet fascinating plot worthy of Vautrin's inventiveness. The tone is more melodramatic than somber in the first two parts of the novel, but suddenly modulates to a much darker mood at the end, when, in a remarkably effective example of foreshortening, Lucien is arrested: "At midnight Lucien was brought to the Force prison . . . where he was put into solitary confinement; the abbé Carlos Herrera had been there since the time of his arrest." This stark sentence, cancelling out the whole previous forward-moving plot line, brings us back into the blunt world of legality and courts: a mystery story becomes a *fait divers*.

Part III is a mixture of digressions on the legal system and the story of Lucien's last days: he comes to life again as he prepares to commit suicide, unaware of the powerful forces that are being marshalled to set him free. The dramatic ironies which have pursued him from the beginning recur for the last time. But the last chapter of Part III, in which the report of Lucien's death is falsified so that it will not appear to be a suicide, brings us back to the ironic maxim Vautrin has always held: "Only appearances count," and in Part IV his sudden ascension from the role of banker for criminals to the position of head of the secret police is Balzac's most striking example of moral ambiguity. The peculiar reversals of plot, and differences in tone among its parts make *Splendeurs et Misères* one of Balzac's most curious achievements. Many chapters of it have the pure entertainment value we have seen in Stendhal: plot becomes a fascinating puzzle, far more intricate than life, and the reader is as often obliged to see over the characters as he is to feel with them. The grotesque masks—Peyrade got up as an Englishman or Vautrin's aunt in her various costumes—contribute to the feeling of play and theater which reduces our involvement in them. In short, parts of *Splendeurs et Misères*, along with certain provincial novels like the sequence *La Vieille Fille-Le Cabinet des antiques*, show us at times a genuinely comic novelist, who expresses himself not through clumsy puns or weird similes but with a certain droll lightness of touch.

The sequence *Goriot-Illusions-Splendeurs et Misères* can be considered, I think, the centripetal point of *La Comédie humaine*. Balzac himself kept classifying and reclassifying his works in a largely arbitrary manner;

if, however, we look for some central thread in the
novel cycle, it would seem to be the old aristocracy,
which occupies the heights others are trying to scale.
It is as if the bourgeoisie, Bohemia, and even the lower
classes formed concentric rings around the traditional
seat of power. The unity of *La Comédie humaine*, insofar as it can be said to have one, depends on unexpected
relations between social classes, whether these take the
form of patronage, as when doctors, lawyers, and judges
penetrate into the *grand monde*, or assume a purely
aggressive character, as when Lucien or Nucingen forces
his way into privileged circles.

From around 1834 to 1840 Balzac carried about in
his head an immense repertoire of characters ranging
from the old nobility to the *haute bourgeoisie* (César
Birotteau is an example), down to the journalistic, theatrical world of Bixiou, Lousteau, and the rest.[5] As a result his shorter pieces tended to become more and more
the kind of accessory narrative I have mentioned in
connection with *Goriot*. *L'Interdiction* (1836), which
deals with Mme d'Espard, her attempt to have her husband declared mentally incompetent, and the subsequent
unmasking of her motives, is an excellent example of
the peculiar relations of the incidental works to the
long novels. (Balzac conceived various tales well before
he wrote them so that the dates of publication do not
correspond to the internal chronology of *La Comédie
humaine*.) The events of *L'Interdiction* are tied in with
those of *Goriot*, since in the opening scene (set in 1828)
Rastignac and Bianchon recall their days at the Pension
Vauquer nine years before. However, in Part II of

---

[5] There even exist dictionaries of Balzac's world, the best known
of which is Anatole Cerfbeer and Jules Christophe, *Répertoire de la
"Comédie humaine"* (Paris, 1888).

Illusions perdues (around 1821), the episode has not yet taken place. Toward 1828, the period of the first part of *Splendeurs et Misères*, Mme d'Espard's difficulties with the law are the subject of gossip. Thus *L'Interdiction* takes place between the scenes, so to speak, of the two longer novels: it clarifies them while not being completely independent of them. There is a kind of mutual interaction of the plots on each other.

Something must now be said of the novels set in the provinces, since several of them, such as *Le Curé de Tours*, *Eugénie Grandet*, and *La Rabouilleuse* are among Balzac's most satisfying and original works. The provincial novels tend to be connected with the Parisian nucleus of *La Comédie humaine* by the device of a character, familiar from the Paris novels, who, for one reason or another, is obliged to visit a provincial town or to maintain relations with a country relative. These works form the periphery of Balzac's world and can, therefore, be read and understood with little reference to the Parisian novels, although they gain in resonance from an acquaintance with the urban, central scheme of *La Comédie humaine*. What they demonstrate above all, however, is that Balzac's fiction is spatially as elaborate as it is chronologically: simultaneity is a spatial concept as well as a temporal one, and the configuration of *La Comédie humaine* must be described at once in both dimensions. Events have a geographical as well as a temporal prolongation, as when the detention of a poor pharmacist's son from Angoulême threatens to bring about the fall of a Minister.

Balzac's originality in shaping his fiction is very apparent: the recurring character, the shifts of point of view among the novels, his handling of fictional time, and the concept of a cycle of novels are all techniques which continued to influence writers for decades after his death. It is essentially from him that realist fiction in France derived. However, there is something paradoxical about Balzac's work: his writing is often careless or tasteless, his interventions embarassing. Rarely, I should think, has a great writer had so many flaws, which is to say that Balzac's greatness is of a very special kind: general technical achievements far outweigh failures of local texture. Flaubert was very much aware of Balzac's strengths and weaknesses, and his conviction that style was the major problem in fiction to be solved seems, in part, to come from his reading of the older novelist: he wrote in a letter of 1852, at a time when the style of *Madame Bovary* was a daily problem for him, "I feel the novel is just being born; it awaits its Homer. What an amazing man Balzac would have been, if only he had known how to write. That's the only thing he lacked. But an artist wouldn't have accomplished so much or had his scope." [6]

[6] Letter of December 17, 1852, to Louise Colet.

3

Minor Genres
Romance and Confession
Novel

THE NOVELS OF STENDHAL AND BALZAC bring up certain questions of technique which are pertinent to subsequent developments in fiction, even though, as is especially the case of Stendhal, they cannot be considered as "influences" in any probable or speculative fashion. We have seen that Stendhal makes considerable use of the conventions of heroic romance, and Balzac, in his subgroup of works called *Etudes philosophiques*, moves away from realism toward the supernatural and the *conte philosophique*. *La Peau de chagrin* (1831), for example, is a story based on the proposition that will at once fulfills man and physically destroys him: each act of power is a step toward death, life a slow suicide. This rather striking and poetic idea suggests the basic difference between the realist novel and what we might call romance; the latter reveals metaphysical truths rather than psychological or social ones. Of course, realistic elements, such as descriptions of actual places, are hardly precluded: *La Peau de Chagrin*, to return to our example, has very evocative passages about the Palais-Royal and the Quai Voltaire. But what happens to Ra-

phaël Valentin illustrates a philosophical interpretation
of life which he is arbitrarily obliged to face, and not a
natural consequence of his personality. It is also characteristic of what we are here calling romance—and a
rather sinister form of it in Balzac—that, as the protagonist becomes distinctly symbolic, usual modes of narration are abandoned: in *La Peau de chagrin*, the great
encyclopedic visions of human history, knowledge, and
vanity have a purely thematic rather than a narrative
function.

Above all, the supernatural can be accommodated
in romance, especially if it takes the form of an ineluc-
table destiny foretold. It is frequently in a superstitious
manner that fate is unveiled: the omen, the stars, the
gypsies' cards. It is obviously impossible to separate
completely the strains of realism and romance in much
fiction, but there are a number of works in the nineteenth century which form a sustained tradition of romance by their themes and by the way these are rendered. Fate is a recurrent motif, but before entering into
this, a further distinction must be made: there is a sense
of fatality in a work like *Illusions perdues*, where the
inevitable quirks of Lucien's character determine his
destiny, as well as do a number of historico-sociological
factors—if journalism were not venal and debased,
would Lucien have been a writer of merit? The question
remains perhaps an open one, but there is no doubt that
a scientific—as opposed to a metaphysical—determinism
brings about Lucien's changes of fortune and final
plight. The supernatural plays no role in this wasted
life. And later on in the century, when we consider
realist novels by Flaubert and Zola, we shall have again
to make this distinction between the fatality of individual
personalities, which their authors considered almost a

medical matter, and the grander, more frightening idea of inexplicable, irremediable doom.

After the *Etudes philosophiques*, which contain probably the greatest range of metaphysical themes dealing with will, matter, and intellect, the novels of Victor Hugo, which span most of the century, are the best known romances to the general reading public. "Ananké" or fate is written on one of the stones of Notre-Dame de Paris, and Hugo's work about the church and the Middle Ages exemplifies his peculiar concept of the novel, which can be found again in *Les Misérables, Les Travailleurs de la mer*, and elsewhere. Hugo's fiction is full of anagogical figures (demons, angels, slaves, heroes) as well as plot lines which, despite their general drift toward fatality, are constantly interrupted by fascinating little essays on such topics as octopus or *l'adoration perpétuelle*. Encyclopedic patterns we have mentioned with regard to Balzac, but Hugo, with his peculiar stylistic brilliance (one not to everyone's taste, to be sure), succeeded in making of his romances treasure-troves of the unexpected and little known. Hugo seems not to have cared about general problems in fictional illusion; rather, he emphasized detail and local color: it is almost possible to open his romances at random and, ignoring the plot, find interesting passages.

Flaubert's *Salammbô* (1862) is another work dominated by fatality, but, while it doubtless owes a great deal to Hugo's example for its range of vocabulary and exotic setting, it is conceived in a fairly strict literary form. *Salammbô* is a prose epic, complete with Homeric similes, and the last sentence: "Thus died Hamilcar's daughter for having touched Tanit's mantle" obviously echoes the last line of the *Iliad*: "Thus they buried horse-taming Hector." The content of *Salammbô* be-

over a humble fire of underbrush, which he had lit in a clear spot in the woods.

In daytime I strayed over vast heaths edged by forests. My reveries needed so little aliment: a dry leaf borne before me on the wind, a cottage from which smoke rose into the bare heights of trees, moss on an oak trunk shivering in the north wind, a remote outcrop of stone, an isolated pond where the dry reed rustles.

At night, when the north wind battered my thatched cottage, when torrential rains fell on my roof and through my window I saw the moon furrow the banked clouds, like some pale vessel ploughing the waves, it seemed to me that life grew doubly intense in my heart, that I could create worlds.

The intense subjectivity of these passages, their lyrical solipsism, is especially heightened, as in the last of our examples, when the speaker moves from the contemplation of nature and pathetic fallacy to imagining he can create a world in his own image. René's concern for his inner world is complemented by a certain vagueness about place and time: we know, of course, about his travels in Italy and Scotland, his remove to America, but the parts of France where so much of his personal drama occurs remain uncertain. Perhaps the greatest underlying thematic principle follows from René's subjectivity: he is steadily frustrated by experience and yet believes experience rather than his interpretation of it to be at fault. *René*, however, is a framed narration in which Father Souël, the missionary, does not fail to point this out. Later confession novels will not always contain a rebuttal of the main character's convictions.

The eighteenth-century antecedents for the confessional genre could perhaps be traced back to *Manon Lescaut* and even beyond, but the works most relevant for nineteenth-century authors are Rousseau's *La Nouvelle Héloïse* and *Confessions*, which complement each other in a curious fashion. The distinction between fiction and reminiscence seems oddly blurred when one compares the style, vagueness of plot line, and emotive content of these works. It is as if Rousseau, by sheer eloquence, managed to fuse autobiography and fiction into an appealing but quite ambiguous texture. One result of this will be a new freedom in the use of letters in frankly fictional contexts: we realize that there is a profound connection between the ordinary first-person narrative and the epistolary form. The nineteenth-century confession novel is characterized by this mingling of truth and fiction, which earlier writers had attempted, by their conventions, to keep distinct. Furthermore, the nineteenth-century genre is so consistent in its stylistic tendencies and thematics that, as we shall see, a parody of it was inevitable: *Mademoiselle de Maupin*.

René is a short narrative, but later confession novels are often lengthy: Musset's *Confessions d'un enfant du siècle* is substantial, to say nothing of Sainte-Beuve's *Volupté*, or Fromentin's *Dominique*, which run on for well over three hundred pages. Senancour's *Obermann* is an example of a rather plotless, epistolary "novel" which also conforms to a confessional pattern. Poets seem to have been especially attracted to the genre: besides the works of Musset and Sainte-Beuve we have mentioned, there are Nerval's pieces of fiction (to be discussed later) and Lamartine's *Graziella*, which confirms our impression of a confusion between autobiography and fiction, in that it was published both as a novel and as a part of Lamartine's memoirs *Les Confidences*. Even Balzac, despite his customary allegiance to third-person narration, dabbled with the confession genre in *Le Lys dans la vallée*, creating a somewhat Chateaubrianesque descriptive style.

Briefly stated, the confession novel is structurally a relatively free genre: letters can mingle with ordinary first-person narrative, and other devices, such as interspersed theatrical dialogue or authorial third-person accounts, can be found. (George Sand's *Lélia* is a relevant example of such casualness in narrative style.) This looseness of form is accompanied by a relaxed conception of plot: the story is presented as autobiography and has the lack of rigor in depiction of events we find in life itself. We see here again a reflection of the eighteenth-century notion of realism: the vicissitudes of ordinary life are supposed to be convincing in a way that a well-structured plot could never be.

But it is perhaps the emotive tenor of the confession novel that best characterizes it: a quite humorless involvement in private feelings, a generally eloquent style, and a concern less for incident than for reactions to incident mark it. Irony is by and large the tone most foreign to confession—in *René*, for example, the author's disapproving point of view is obscured under the weight of gorgeous prose—but there is one significant example of a parody of the confessional genre, *Mademoiselle de Maupin* (1835), one of the most original works of French fiction in the romantic period.

The seventeen chapters of this narrative (it would be an exaggeration to call it a novel) cover the space of a vague winter, late spring, summer, and early autumn in some indeterminate *ancien régime* town during an indeterminate year. The setting is Henri IV-Louis XIII or, as we would say today, baroque.

An important part of the ironic structure of *Made-*

moiselle de Maupin consists in the frequent shifting from epistolary confession to a semiomniscient (or coyly omniscient) third-person narration, and occasionally even to dramatic dialogue. The subdivisions of these narrative points of view are furthermore multiple: in introducing letters or in straight narrative, the authorial voice is quite capable of telling us everything we want to know or else, at other times, nothing. The author constantly plays with conventions to show that the confessor-hero, d'Albert, is a fool, but a fool redeemed by the esthete within him. In the usual confession novel—let's say *René* after the hero of which d'Albert is modeled—the protagonist is a lyrical and completely solipsistic voice speaking to us of his own inability to love or to achieve his ideal of art; d'Albert, on the other hand, through the author's manipulations of point of view, becomes obviously deceived and self-deceiving. The sexual identity and tastes of the characters are the principal objects of the author's irony, but, to a somewhat lesser degree, d'Albert's inability to reconcile his highly esthetic view of life with reality—expressed in prose whose poetic elegance is such that we only intermittently see it as the author's parodic idiom—provides the novel with its characteristic voluptuous tone and vagueness with regard to the characters' psychology.

It is important to note that chronology is haphazardly indicated in the work, except insofar as we know that its central action occurs in the course of a summer spent in the country: there d'Albert and his mistress Rosanette both covet Théodore—unbeknownst to them, a young woman in male costume. The focus of the narrative is not produced by temporal heightening, such as we might encounter in Balzac, but by a mirror image of the action: the plot of *As You Like It*, which the inhabitants of the chateau perform. All sexual ambiguities are emphasized, and the book concludes with Théodore, the female-male sent by Venus, satisfying in the same night both d'Albert and Rosanette.

The impudicity of all this is skillfully gotten around by a style which is constantly appealing in its sumptuousness and by the fact that *Mademoiselle de Maupin* is a fable about art and life coinciding for one glorious moment. Underneath the parody of the confession novel lies an elaborate thematic complex dealing with the superiority of esthetic experiences over all others and the decay of art from its Hellenic perfections to the present. In other words, the levity of the mock confession is used to keep the more serious side of the work from seeming pompous or poorly adapted to a narrative genre, as when Hellenic esthetics are invoked to justify d'Albert's supposedly being a homosexual. Seriousness constantly hides behind levity.

Mademoiselle de Maupin is a curious example of a book which, by the elegance of its parody, eclipses the power of the works which it mimics (*Don Quixote's* place in literature must be seen in like terms). Gautier's inventions are such that one hardly needs to know the vulgar species of confession novel in order to appreciate this transmogrification of it. There is another novel, however, which, while belonging broadly to the confessional genre, remains distinct from the ordinary run of it by its stylistic achievement and complexity of narrative method: Nerval's *Sylvie* (1854) which, while deriving from commonplace narrative patterns, constitutes a completely new departure in the quest for subtle rendering of the sense of time.

Nerval's *Aurélia*, whose form was inspired by the *Vita Nuova*, is better known in general than *Sylvie*, since its narrative has more relevance to the interpretation of Nerval's verse, but *Sylvie* remains not only Nerval's most complex example of fictional technique, but one of the most interesting ones in mid-nineteenth-century France. The plot of *Sylvie* is, on the surface, so modest that it can be easily assimilated to the confessional-autobiographical genre. However, there are complicated time patterns, ambiguities of meaning, and symbolic detail which make of it a very convoluted example of narration. *Sylvie* begins on a "lost night" when the narrator has been to the theater in Paris to admire an actress he loves, a passion of which she is unaware. His thoughts, as he is coming home, revolve around the historical past: the late eighteenth century; Rome in the time of Apuleius, rhetors, and sophists; the subterranean gods worshipped in Alexandria; Moloch; and Druid rituals, as well as many others. These help to transport the reader from an urban setting in a period of "renovation and decadence" to the ancient and pastoral motifs of the narrator's memories of his youth and to the mysteries inherent in them. The peculiarly allusive, evocative, and associative qualities of this prose bring it close to rather modern kinds of poetic style or to the opening pages of *A la recherche du temps perdu.*

He first recalls a baroque chateau in the Valois and a blond girl, Adrienne, of noble birth, who sang in a regional fête, who resembled Beatrice, and who, a year later, was destined to convent life. Chapter 3 next compares the future nun of yesterday with the actress, and in very peculiar terms: "Supposing they were the same woman!" An odd notion at best, but which will underly the whole story. This leads, by antithesis, to the memory of the narrator's other provincial love, Sylvie. At once he sets off for the Valois in the middle of the night, knowing that the local festival (August 24, Saint Bartholomew's Day), which he has seen announced in a Paris newspaper, will still be in progress.

Here we must first consider the peculiar time planes of the narrative. We have a series of present-time episodes separated by scenes taking place at various periods in the past. And finally the present-tense episodes at the end of the work go beyond the present of the beginning, even though we are not made especially aware of temporal lapse. Casual connective sentences move us in and out of present time, although seldom clarifying its chronology. Parts IV, V, and VI deal with a recent past—situated between childhood memories of Adrienne and the present—at a time when a trip to Loisy includes a Watteau-like *voyage à Cythère*. On that occasion the then adolescent narrator crowns Sylvie, as he had Adrienne in a more remote past. Next, after seeing the convent where the narrator imagines Adrienne to be, he dresses up, along with Sylvie, in *ancien régime* wedding costumes that the latter's aunt had saved. Love for Adrienne and Sylvie is thus juxtaposed, somewhat like the sacred and profane love allegories of the Renaissance. The possibility of marriage with Sylvie is countered by his faithfulness to the memory of Adrienne.

A brief return to the present (night, and the coach trip to Loisy) is followed by an episode situated in an indefinite past time, not before all previous events but somewhere in between them. The thematic link is Saint Bartholomew's Day, and the content is a visit with Sylvie's brother (she is not there) to a private fête, occurring on the same date as the local village holiday. Adrienne and other convent girls perform a medieval mystery play. The peculiarity of the episode comes from the fact that, after telling it, the narrator begins to wonder if it had been a dream, whether Adrienne was really there. Since Sylvie was absent and her brother was drunk, the chances of determining the reality of the incident are slight. The very fact, however, of mysterious recollections in the narrator's mind suggests that the underlying theme is a contrast between what seems to be reality and an intuitive truth beneath it.

At this point we must note some subtleties of tense and time plane in *Sylvie*. The opening pages are largely in the imperfect tense, suggesting some remoteness from *now*: "We were living, in those days . . . ." But as the narrator's return to Loisy takes place, a present-tense interior monologue is used: "Fortunately I'm leaving the realm of dreams and have only a fifteen-minute walk to get to Loisy . . . ." The next sentences confirm that the narrator is using the conversational past tense: "Je suis entré au bal de Loisy . . . ." The ambiguity between the preterite tense (*J'entrai*), with its looser relation to the present, and the *passé composé*, which often functions as a present perfect, is exploited by Nerval in order to move up and down the time line with great freedom. The use of present and present perfect tenses to achieve interior monologue in a first-person narrative is rather rare in this period and makes of Nerval something of an innovator.

There is a further time pattern in *Sylvie* which use of tenses cannot describe. This is the distinction between the sacral period of earlier memories, which have metaphysical meaning, and the secular time of mere events and causality, which informs the second half of the work. As soon as the narrator arrives at Loisy, the contrast between the enchanted past and the mediocre present becomes apparent. Sylvie has turned into a sophisticated *petite bourgeoise*, who has read *La Nouvelle*

Héloïse and sings operatic arias. She has given up her métier as lacemaker (an old and refined trade) to sew gloves. "Save me," the narrator implores, not realizing immediately that she is engaged to an apprentice pastry-cook, his foster brother. A second time after the local fête he refuses to sleep (Nerval makes a number of these structural repetitions to avoid a disjointed effect in his narrative). And he can no longer find "anything of the past" in Sylvie's parents' house. Even the old aunt has died.

As the narrator becomes more and more discouraged by the "modernity" of his old friends, he begins to remember Adrienne. Here arises one of the most subtle ambiguities in the plot: questioned about Adrienne by the narrator, Sylvie becomes angry and refuses to say more than that "Things turned out badly." Time then elapses as the narrator removes to Germany in order to write a play. Through theatrical contacts he meets the actress of the beginning of *Sylvie*: her name is Aurélie, she accepts him as a lover, and eventually the troupe she is with goes to the towns in the Valois which have been the setting of the preceding episodes.

He seizes this occasion to tell Aurélie about Adrienne, which promptly enrages her: "You don't love me! You are expecting me to say that the actress is the same person as the nun. You're looking for a plot, that's all, and don't know how to end it." The narrator's reflection near the beginning becomes a dramatic element. It is curious that in a narrative so devoid of traditional mechanisms of plot, a main character should reproach the narrator for trying to find one, but this also ties in with Sylvie's "Things turned out badly." Can the actress really, literally, be the nun, having escaped her cloister, or is the identification of the two merely symbolic? On the plane of realistic narration, Adrienne, if she is indeed the former nun, would have every reason to hide her past. The question receives at least a narrative conclusion: when Sylvie, who has been invited by the narrator to Aurélie's performance, is questioned about resemblances between the latter and Adrienne, she merely laughs and remarks that Adrienne died some time before, in 1832.

The question of the oneness of Adrienne and Aurélie is never really investigated, and the only person who could enlighten the narrator about the identity of Adrienne-Aurélie is Sylvie, who will reveal nothing. In other words, we have in *Sylvie* a striking example of a narrator who does not know all the facts in the story he is telling, and an author who hides behind his narrator: the latter does his best to make sense out of the oddments of information at his disposition; but there remains a mystery concealed beneath.

First-person narration proved to be a pitfall for many writers, however skillfully it was handled by others. For Flaubert, who had used it in his juvenilia, it became something almost equivalent to bad technique. His conception of "impersonal" narration surely owes a great debt, by reaction, to the penchant for losing oneself in subjective reminiscences, to the logical and emotive blindness that confessional narration could encourage. Flaubert's search for a new method of narrating has, as we can see from his correspondence, almost an ethical imperative about it, and it produced the first whole theory and practice of fictional technique in the history of the European novel.

4

Flaubert
His Disciples and Impersonal Narration

FLAUBERT'S HABIT OF THINKING quite consciously, as he slowly wrote his novels, about the alternatives which lay before him in style and the structure of narrative units gave his books a kind of consistency and finish which was new. It is obvious from Balzac's review of *La Chartreuse de Parme* that he too had some broad notions about the novel, but they never attained the generality of expression that we find in the literary observations in Flaubert's correspondence. In a sense we can trace the whole idea of experimentation in fiction back to Flaubert, and it is reasonable to say that he lies at the beginning of the twentieth-century conception of fiction as a complex genre which needs constant rethinking: James, Joyce, and countless others are indebted to Flaubert's obsessive concern with defining and refining his chosen genre.

Flaubert's defining and refining were part of a lengthy and quite self-conscious development as a writer. Unlike Balzac, who had no substantial private income, Flaubert was able to fret over his writings for about two decades before *Madame Bovary* (1857), his first publication, made him a public—even notorious—figure. The first genre which he tried was the confession novel: *Mémoires d'un fou* (1838) and *Novembre* (1842) are sometimes tedious, but not lengthy, exercises in Chateaubrianesque style and wandering plot structure. The fact that Flaubert never published these works bespeaks the great seriousness of his vocation and his determination, first of all, as he wrote, "to please myself." In 1843–45, with the first *Education sentimentale* (which has no resemblance to the one of 1869), Flaubert made a great step forward in the theory of his art. The bulk of the work is the story of two young men living in a rather fancy pension in Paris and of their philosophical and emotive coming to maturity. One has an affair with a married woman; the other discovers the secret of literary greatness, and the book concludes with a long rumination on art as self-sacrifice, an indictment of autobiographical fiction, and the affirmation that style alone confers perdurable beauty to writing. In one important way this passage shows a supersession of Flaubert's early esthetic ideals: the notion of style replaces any concern for art as the expression of the individual sensibility; the confession novel yields to third-person narrative, and an attempt to substitute scene for effusion, "objectivity" for tirade. Of course, the idea of objectivity in narrative is a completely impossible one, as Flaubert's later correspondence occasionally and deviously admits, but the degree of the formal expression of objectivity still varies greatly, and Flaubert was correct in assuming that a new texture in fiction could be created with objectivity in mind. The first *Education sentimentale*, however well it expresses this notion, contains, nevertheless, abundant examples of authorial butting-in and none too much of the free indirect discourse that was later to be a major stylistic tool in reducing the novelist's obtrusive role in his works.

Madame Bovary has a very Balzacian subtitle: *Moeurs de province*. And Flaubert expressed the fear that the novel would be nothing more than "Chateaubrianized Balzac." It would certainly be imperceptive to underestimate the influence of Balzac in *Madame Bovary*: the lengthy and discursive description of Yonville at the beginning of Part II of the novel is a good example of this, as is the immense documentary background about real facts, such as the rectification of a clubfoot, which Flaubert generously supplies. On the other hand, Flaubert's novel does not resemble, in its texture, any work in *La Comédie humaine*: Balzac's influence has been combined with a wide range of new techniques, which include not only the care for evocative vocabulary and eloquent rhythms that the term *du Balzac chateaubrianisé* implies, but also a new conception of narrative method. *Bovary* would indeed have been simply a Balzac novel written in lush prose had Flaubert not completely renewed fictional technique.

Flaubert made three major innovations in writing *Bovary*: the abundant use of free indirect discourse, recurrent imagery, and the invention of striking chapter forms. Of these, free indirect discourse is perhaps the most important for the subsequent history of fictional technique. We might best begin by contrasting it with the devices earlier novelists used to convey a character's inner life.

We have had occasion to call effects like the monologue in Stendhal, the overheard conversation in Balzac, and the dialogue in parts of *Mademoiselle de Maupin* devices more suitable to theater than to prose fiction:

never in Flaubert, however, do we feel that an alien genre is determining narrative conventions; free indirect discourse is the technique by which he welds together a character's impressions of the outer world and his subjective interpretations of them. This is perhaps the most complex device by which nineteenth- and twentieth-century novelists have been able to give, in their third-person works, an air of smoothness and continuity. There are already, in the first *Education sentimentale*, a number of examples of this device, and it has been shown that the technique goes back at least as far as La Fontaine, but *Bovary* is unquestionably the first work in which it becomes a major mode of narration.

Free indirect discourse is, on the surface, merely a device for presenting characters' thoughts without the need for such clumsy expedients as monologue: "Julian said to himself: 'my old mother . . .'" or what we might call authorial grammatical intervention: "Julian then thought that it would be better to . . . and that his old mother would be pleased." In free indirect discourse we might have: "Julian thought to desert the army. His old mother would be pleased." In other words, free indirect discourse starts ordinarily with something like a banal "he thought that . . ." but subsequent sentences are free in the sense that they require no verbs of thinking or saying. All this may sound like a petty grammarian's argument until one applies it to fiction since Flaubert: it then becomes apparent that this has endless possibilities for innuendo and ambiguity.[1] We shall now consider three examples of it taken from *Madame Bovary*.

[1] The most thorough study of free indirect discourse and its possibilities is Dorrit Cohn, "Narrated Monologue: Definition of a Fictional Style," *Comparative Literature*, XIII (Spring, 1966), 97–112.

Here is Charles's early upbringing, his mother's struggles with his father over pedagogical principles:

> She had visions of greatness—already seeing him as a grown man, handsome and intelligent, with a settled position in the Highways Department or the Law. She taught him to read, and even to sing two or three little ballads, to the accompaniment of an old piano that she had. All of which was pronounced by Monsieur Bovary, who had little use for culture, to be *so much waste of time*. How would they ever be able to keep the boy at a state school, to buy him a post, or set him up in business: And anyhow, *with a bit of cheek a man can always get on in the world*. Madame Bovary bit her lip, and the boy ran wild in the village.

The language of free indirect discourse can be drawn from any level of style for a desired effect: here Flaubert's use of italics underscores mindless clichés; transitions like *anyhow* belong to the character and not the author, and, finally, the contrast between "visions of greatness" and "the Highways Department" forms a rather tart commentary on the elder Madame Bovary's sense of proportion. The anonymous author sneaks in and out of his characters' heavy stupidity.

A similar ambiguity can be seen in passages where Emma's erotic dreams are described; here the discrepancy is between romantic literature and life: "And yet sometimes it occurred to her that this was the finest time of her life, the so-called honeymoon. To savor all its sweetness one would have to travel to those lands with sonorous names, where wedding morrows have a more delicious indolence. In a post-chaise, behind blue silk curtains, you climb at a walking-pace up steep roads, listening to the postillion's song echoing across the mountain, amid the tinkling of goat-bells and the muffled noise of waterfalls." The interesting thing about this passage is that Emma would be incapable of such luxuriant language and the elegant rhythms of the French text: the lines represent what Emma has read, not what she could express. And at the same time we feel an ironic distance between the author and the banal dreams of romance his character entertains. As in the preceding quotation, Flaubert is toying with the reader's response: pseudo-lyricism is being slipped in much the same way clichés have been before.

Flaubert had a very complex feeling for language. He made an imaginative use of banalities (preserved in his *Dictionnaire des idées reçues*) which is unlike any previous handling of them, with perhaps the exception of a few pages of Stendhal or Balzac. Tasteless, stupid remarks became a staple of Flaubert's style, and have proved to be one of the most enduring of his discoveries: there is an air of reality about Homais' imbecilities that we cannot feel in the rhetoric of the abbé Prévost or Chateaubriand. On the other hand, Flaubert had an intense love of lyricism, which, while checked by his penchant for irony and his maturing taste in prose style, sometimes produced highly poetic passages. These, however, show the same tendency toward ambiguity that we have observed in Flaubert's use of cliché. The most remarkable one in *Bovary*, to my mind, is the description of extreme unction:

> The priest recited the Misereatur and the Indulgentiam; then he dipped his right thumb into the oil and began the unctions: first on the eyes, that had so coveted all earthly splendors; then on the nostrils that had loved warm breezes and amorous perfumes; then on the mouth, that had opened for falsehood, had groaned with pride, and

cried out in lust; then on the hands, that had reveled
in delicious contacts; lastly on the soles of the feet, that
once had run so swiftly to the assuaging of her desires,
and now would walk no more.

The passage is based on a liturgical formula which only
varies in the words for the various parts of the body
which have sinned: "Per istam sanctam Unctionem, et
suam piissimam misericordiam, indulgeat tibi Dominus
quidquid per visum deliquisti." "By this holy unction
and its great mercy, may the Lord forgive all sins that
you have committed through the sense of sight." The
most interesting thing about this passage is the way Flaubert adds to the prayer, with the result that the text
represents less and less what the priest says, but ambig-
uously suggests his words along with a completely different point of view, an erotic and nostalgic one. The
emphasis is on the beauty of sin, not forgiveness. The
eloquent rhythms and evocative phrases are perhaps a
stylization of what is going on in Emma's mind. Or this
might be a somewhat disguised authorial intervention.
It is impossible, and this, I think, is the greatest merit
of the passage, to separate the points of view which are
so subtly interwoven. Flaubert has created a delicate
linguistic instrument which registers at once the formal
ceremony and a kind of anguish at the body's removal
from earthly pleasures which goes beyond one's particular judgment of Emma.

We can now see that Flaubert arrived at the final
version of *Madame Bovary* by juggling and modifying
a number of techniques. In his correspondence he speaks
of moving "imperceptibly" from psychological material
to the "dramatic"; his remarks on the author's absence
from his novel are well known, and he was upset by the
large element of "vulgarity" which must melt into a

"narrative analysis." In other words Flaubert is defining the peculiar quality of the texture of his novel: for the first time description, narration, and inner thoughts fuse together. Through free indirect discourse the borderline between dialogue and telling grows faint and ambiguous. And the whole question of authorial omniscience, with its attendant criticism of lack of verisimilitude, vanishes as the author and character seem to cohere. Flaubert is performing a sleight-of-hand feat which makes the fictional illusion all the more perfect.

The history of the writing of *Madame Bovary*, and the elaboration of techniques involved, has been recorded with fair accuracy.[2] The editors of the "new version" admit that their text represents not any specific complete version but merely a composite of early sketches and later definitive passages. However, this composite is of immense value when one tries to weigh the preponderence of various elements in the putting together of the definitive *Bovary*.

The most important thing perhaps that we find in the new version is the system of related stances, actions, and colors: already Emma is frequently bending to disentangle her skirt, pursing or biting her lips, gazing out of windows, leaning back in a position of passivity, and wearing blue, imagining and admiring blue things. There are, of course, many other such recurrent images in the novel, and one of the most influential aspects of the work is the elaborate interconnection of so many of its parts. No previous novel in French had had anything like the cross-references of *Bovary*, whereas subsequent fiction is full of them. This use of recurrent detail is

[2] Gustave Flaubert, *Madame Bovary: Nouvelle Version, précédée de scénarios inédits,* ed. Jean Pommier and Gabrielle Leleu (Paris, 1947).

often called symbolic, but the term is somewhat pretentious, since the details seldom imply a very stable
pattern of symbolic meaning. For example, the barometer in the Bovarys' house is mentioned twice: it gleams
in the setting sun as Rodolphe comes to call with the
intention of seducing Emma; sometime later, when Emma terminates a period of estrangement from Rodolphe,
because she is infuriated at Charles's stupid mishandling
of the clubfoot operation, she slams a door and sends the
barometer crashing to the floor. The reappearance of the
barometer is an effective device, but it is not easy to
analyze why. The barometer is not a facile symbol:
changes in real atmospheric pressure do not correspond
to Emma's relations with Charles or Rodolphe. There
is no elementary relation between the object and the
emotive ambiance. On the other hand, the conception
of a barometer as a measure of a certain kind of tension
permits its transference to Emma's psychological situation.

Recurrent details in *Bovary* usually function in this
way; their symbolic value is something one feels, and
the explanation of it tends to be indirect and devious.
It is probably more accurate to consider them less as
symbols than as structural devices: they add another dimension to the patterns of time and place which we
have already seen in Balzac and Stendhal. Objects become somehow bound to events or emotive states in an
ambiguous, subtle fashion which makes them, therefore,
all the more striking. The obtrusiveness of cruder forms
of allegory is obviated; these elements are not simplistic
like the dyer's wastes which Zola was to underscore in
L'Assommoir (from pink and blue they change to black
as Gervaise's fortunes decline). Flaubert's repetitions
seem to form a more natural part of the scene of his

narration or to be less portentous, and therefore more powerful, such as Emma's "honeymoon" with Léon in Rouen which discreetly and distantly echoes the meditation on *la lune de miel* which occurs near the beginning of the novel.

The new version also shows us another important fact about Flaubert's imagination: unlike Balzac, who constantly added to his text, fleshing it out and enriching it with appropriate detail,[3] Flaubert's principal concern in working a first draft into a finished version was to cut out, to blue pencil excessive developments and extraneous facts. Much of his laconic tone and many abrupt juxtapositions can be traced to this. The kind of writing Flaubert felt most obliged to excise was witty and venomous presentations of the obiter dicta of Bovary *père* and, most of all, of Homais. Flaubert was endlessly fertile in writing imbecilic dialogue, but he recognized that too much of it would completely unbalance his book.

There is, however, another kind of passage in which excision proved valuable. Here is the final version of the description of the old duke at the house party at La Vaubyessard:

> At the head of the table, alone among all those women, sat one aged man, crouched over his plate, with his napkin tied round his neck like a bib, dribbling gravy as he ate. His eyes were bloodshot, and he wore a little pigtail tied with black ribbon. This was the Marquis' father-in-law, the old Duc de Laverdière, once the favorite of the Comte d'Artois in the days of the Marquis de Conflans' hunting-parties at Le Vaudreuil; he was said to have been the lover of Marie Antoinette, between Messieurs de

---

[3] The early versions of the first part of *Illusions perdues* have been published and are a fascinating testimony to Balzac's writing habits. See Honoré de Balzac, *Illusions perdues*, ed. Suzanne-Jean Bernard (Paris, 1959).

Coigny and de Lauzun. He had filled his life with riot
and debauch, with duels, wagers, and abductions; had
squandered his wealth and been the terror of his family.
He pointed to the dishes, mumbling, and a footman
stationed behind him named them aloud in his ear. Emma's
eyes kept turning in spite of themselves towards that old
man with the drooling lips, as though to some august
curiosity. He had lived at Court, had lain in the Queen's
bed!

We feel a certain break between the sentence ending
"terror of his family" and the one beginning with "He
pointed to the dishes." This lack of logical sequence
for ironic effect is one of Flaubert's most characteristic
devices, yet he only discovered it in the course of re-
writing. Originally there had been five intervening and
unmotivated sentences which sketched out the duke's
life between the Revolution and the present, and termi-
nated with transitional phrases about his still-lingering
love of food and his place in his son-in-law's household.
The early version demonstrates Flaubert's indebtedness
to Balzac's meaty chunks of exposition, the later one
Flaubert's becoming himself. And the paragraph terminates with one of those delicate effects whereby one
suddenly passes from an anonymous narration into a
character's consciousness. Strictly speaking, Emma
would know little about the old duke, but we feel no
lack of verisimilitude—so subtle are Flaubert's transitions—where her inner exclamation rounds off the paragraph.

Another very effective device that Flaubert invented
even after he had finished the text of *Madame Bovary*
was that of his chapter patterns. It seems almost incred-
ible that so elegantly structured a book as *Bovary* could
have been planned without an eye to chapter form. Yet
all evidence indicates that he never bothered with the

problem until the novel was to appear in serial form. On the other hand, the book was obviously written with a strong feeling for contrasting episodes, which the ultimate division into chapters merely formalizes: many chapters consist of two antithetical parts, such as Chapter 7, Part II, in which the departure of Léon is followed by Rodolphe's first appearance. Another, and similar, structural device is the juxaposition of two interior monologues: after Charles has bungled the clubfoot operation, he and Emma each sit quietly thinking—he about his failure, she about his mediocrity—and we pass, in the succession of paragraphs, from the thoughts of the one to those of the other. We have already seen this technique of a shifting point of view in Balzac, as when Poiret and Mlle Michonneau talk to the police without Rastignac being present, but Flaubert systematically exploits the possibiltites of the technique, whereas Balzac seems more to happen on it unpremeditatedly.

The writing of *Bovary* was, as we have said, accompanied by many theoretical statements about the novel, some of which are famous, such as the idea of the book "about nothing" which style alone would hold together, or the comparison of the novelist with God in the universe, everywhere present but invisible. There remained, however, a considerable gap between theory and practice, for we find in *Bovary* some intrusions that force the reader to notice the author as a personality. These are not necessarily awkward and are sometimes quite apposite, as in the following passage where we pass from Rodolphe's thoughts about Emma to Flaubert's reflections on language: "Because wanton or mercenary lips had murmured like phrases in his ear, he had but scant belief in the sincerity of these. High-flown language concealing tepid affection must be discounted, thought

he: as though the full heart may not sometimes overflow
in the emptiest metaphors, since no one can ever give
the exact measure of his needs, his thoughts, or his sor-
rows, and human speech is like a cracked kettle on
which we beat out tunes to make a bear dance, when
we would move the stars to pity." Here Flaubert is both
stating the technical problem which led him into irony
and indirection and showing how close he remained to
the metaphoric style of the romantics: his subsequent
development was to take him away from any so color-
ful an image and into a style in which *grisaille* or mono-
chrome was to dominate. I am speaking of *L'Education
sentimentale* (1869) and "Un Coeur simple" (1877).
But before we examine this later phase of Flaubert's
realistic art, there is a period of transition in French
fiction between 1857 and 1877 which we must now
turn our attention to.

Baudelaire sketched out an article on realism, which
he never wrote, but which has some interestingly sar-
donic remarks on the use of the word in the 1850s and
what meaning, "if at all," it had. He deals mostly with
the esthetic ideas (rather vague ones at that) of the
minor writers Champfleury and Duranty, who made
the term *realism* better known in literary circles than
it had been before. Treating of what was realistic, they
emphasized simplicity of style and everydayness of subject. But such abstract formulations should not deceive
us: Duranty's most enduring fame comes from his review, in the short-lived periodical *Le Réalisme*, of *Madame Bovary*, which he found to be "materialistic,"
overly descriptive, and lacking in "feeling." The most
sentimental romantic could hardly have put it better.
Duranty's realism avoids irony in favor of the morally

uplifting. The complex texture of *Madame Bovary* he understood not at all.

It is more revealing perhaps to analyze the work of the Goncourt brothers, because of their genuine efforts to create a new kind of fiction and because of the esteem in which they were held by novelists who were their contemporaries. In the last decade of Flaubert's life a group of disciples or associates formed about him; they included Zola, Daudet, Huysmans, Maupassant, and Edmond de Goncourt, who was only one year younger than the master himself. The Goncourts (Jules died in 1870 and consequently did not belong to the Flaubert circle) set out to create a kind of fiction which would be free of falseness and self-complacency. Their most famous statement of aims is contained in the preface to *Germinie Lacerteux* (1864), where they insist on the importance of writing truthful novels about the proletariat. This may seem a bit pretentious coming two years after *Les Misérables*, but the Goncourts had their point to make: Hugo's proletarian characters are part of a vast web in which their lives merely reflect the larger design of the conflict between good and evil— Jean Valjean represents evil redeemed through love, and so forth. *Germinie Lacerteux*, on the other hand, attempts an objective account of the life of a housemaid, who, having fallen in love with a worthless young man, declines and dies after passing through deceit, lust, and alcoholism. It is important to compare *Germinie Lacerteux* with *Madame Bovary* in order to see how, with a certain conception of realism in common, Flaubert wrote a great book and the Goncourts a literary curiosity. To begin with, their attitudes toward their characters are similar—discreetly sympathetic, but informed by a grim sense of socioeconomic determinism—yet their fictional techniques differ greatly. *Germinie Lacerteux* is not one of the Goncourts' novels where stylistic eccentricity is everywhere, but it does show their typical insensitivity to narrative form: many chapters are only a sketchy page or two long; most of them have no coherence as subdivisions of a whole. One never has the feeling that a chapter is built around one or two carefully prepared scenes. There is far more telling than showing as it was later to be called, and somehow the showing never seems put at the right affective moment of the story. Flaubert's concern for tableaux or narrative analysis is missing. And, finally, little essaylike paragraphs—rather less compelling than those of Balzac, although resembling them in their grotesque pseudoscience—distract one's attention. "This happy and unsatisfied love produced in Germinie's physical being a peculiar physiological phenomenon. It seemed as if passion, circulating within her, renewed and transformed her lymphatic balance" (Chapter 10). I doubt that this would have seemed scientifically grounded even in 1864.

Between Champfleury and Duranty's polemics over realism and the examples of Flaubert and the Goncourts, younger writers like Zola were becoming aware of a new orientation in fiction. But for the great exemplar of the new novel they had to await the publication, in 1869, of *L'Education sentimentale*. For its influence on younger writers we need only quote Huysmans, reminiscing years later in the 1903 preface to *A rebours*: "This school [naturalism] seldom portrayed exceptional characters, at least in theory. It limited itself to the depiction of average lives and tried, on the pretext of reproducing reality, to create characters which would resemble most of us. This goal was attained in a masterpiece which, far more than *L'Assommoir*, was the model of naturalism: *L'Education sentimentale;* this book was for us all a veritable bible." And Zola was to regret that Flaubert had died before the completion of *Pot-Bouille*, Zola's bourgeois novel, which derives from *L'Education* in its cool prose and its use of prostitution as a metaphor for nineteenth-century society.[4]

The flowing Seine seems often in *L'Education sentimentale* to represent the dreariness of ebbing time; the boat journey which Frédéric takes in the first chapter prepares us for a kind of imitative form in which events will occur in a rhythm which is the opposite of Balzac's precipitous time dimension: they come and go with no sense of excitement; the anonymous narrator propels us forward but does not comment at any length on the passing scenery.[5] However, this is only part of a complex of representations of time which inform the novel. The work contains an ironic picture of successive historical events which never seem to touch the main character at the right moment: Frédéric's sluggish inner time never meshes with coarse reality, and Flaubert takes great pains to establish an odd counterpoint between historic reality and Frédéric's subjective awareness. Furthermore, the novel has a peculiar plot structure which corresponds to Frédéric's always being out of step with reality. A brief résumé of the earlier chapters will demonstrate the curiously negative character of their contents. Still full of his meeting on the boat with the Arnoux—Monsieur is a new friend; Madame he adores—Frédéric arrives in Paris to study law and make his fortune, perhaps through a letter of introduction

---

[4] See Brombert, *Flaubert*, 125–85.

[5] The classic analysis of this, as well as of Flaubert's style, is in Albert Thibaudet, *Gustave Flaubert* (Paris, 1935). For the Seine see p. 141.

to the rich Dambreuse, whose beautiful wife he suspects might even become his mistress. Dambreuse, on meeting Frédéric, has nothing to say to him, while Madame vanishes, apparitionlike, in her carriage. He tries to find Arnoux in his shop but fails. When the Dambreuses do not send the expected invitation, he consoles himself by going to gaze at Mme Arnoux's windows, but she is not there and does not even live there. A certain Sénécal having been recommended to him by his hometown friend Deslauriers, Frédéric tries, in vain, three times to find Sénécal. I pass over a number of minor nonevents. Finally something does happen: an unexpected dinner invitation from Mme Arnoux arrives, but at the same time comes a note from Deslauriers announcing his arrival in Paris on the same evening as the dinner. Here we find a plot device that will complement the negative occurrences in the novel: either nothing happens or else Frédéric is faced with choosing between simultaneous and almost equally enticing prospects. On later occasions he will make the choice between going to see the Dambreuses, who presumably will make his fortune, and visiting Mme Arnoux: the latter option, as usual, wins out, but the visits to Mme Arnoux always turn into dead ends. Passion has dictated Frédéric's choice, but his passion has no purchase on that terribly chaste lady.

Flaubert devised an extraordinary series of nonevents in *L'Education sentimentale*. Failure to find someone after hours of search, misunderstandings (Frédéric, who has broken Arnoux's mistress' parasol, without knowing she is secretly visiting their apartment, offers Mme Arnoux a replacement), and disappointments (at Frédéric's first dinner with the Arnoux, Madame says only one sentence and a very banal one at that). Toward the conclusion of the novel, Frédéric thinks it is Rosanette and not Mme Dambreuse who has Mme Arnoux's furnishings auctioned as a consequence of her husband's bankruptcy, and the final quidproquo occurs when Mme Arnoux asks about Rosanette's portrait: "It's an old Italian painting," Frédéric replies.

We must now examine the larger time patterns in the novel and their relation to the plot structure. Flaubert planned his time-event scheme with absolute accuracy and then avoided any obvious suggestion in his text of such minute planning. He always keeps two time lines going: one is the objective one of history, in which February 1848 or December 1851 are significant political moments; the other time line is psychological and internal. The interplay between the two time planes provides considerable dramatic irony.

Perhaps the best example of this occurs in February 1848. As the time of the Revolution approaches, Flaubert, who, hitherto, has seldom mentioned years or months, suddenly puts the reader on a clear time track, and, as February 22 draws near, stresses even the succession of days. While time thickens and becomes subdivided, place is also more and more emphasized so that, on the afternoon of February 22, 1848, Frédéric is waiting for Mme Arnoux behind the Madeleine on the rue Tronchet, while a crowd of students, audible but hidden by the church, has a rally on the Place de la Madeleine. (The episode is historical.) Yet the reader is more involved with Frédéric's wait for Mme Arnoux and his disappointment. The succeeding days of the Revolution are, for the reader's surface attention, occupied by the beginning of Frédéric's liaison with Rosanette, the shooting in the streets becoming merely an annoyance for the lovers. "Heroes don't smell good," remarks a character after the Tuileries have been taken, and that epitomizes Frédéric's involvement in history. Unlike Frédéric, however, the ideal reader is very much aware of what the "February days" were to mean for French society and can read the episode with an appropriate ironic insight.

A similar densification of time occurs in December 1852, temporal exactitude having been relaxed since the 1848 episodes. The sale of Mme Arnoux's furniture is set for December first, the eve of the anniversary of the Battle of Austerlitz and the day before Napoleon III was to proclaim the Second Empire. Frédéric's tumultuous private life barely permits him to be aware of events, except for the episode, on his return from a brief visit to Nogent, of Sénécal's murdering Dussardier. There is a feeling of public and private chaos which has been building and which culminates in this scene. Time then again becomes liquid and fugitive when Frédéric leaves Paris.

The beginning of the chapter in which Frédéric's later life is recounted is justly famous and demonstrates certain new qualities in Flaubert's prose which differentiate it considerably from that of *Madame Bovary:*

> He traveled.
> He came to know the melancholy of ships, chilly awakenings in tents, dazzling landscapes and ruins, the sorrow of fleeting friendships.
> He returned.
> He moved in society, and he had further love affairs. But the constant memory of the first one made them insipid; and then the violence of desire, the very flower of sensation had been lost. His intellectual ambitions had also declined. Years passed; and he endured his intellectual idleness and the inertia of his heart.

Here Flaubert demonstrates how effective telling rather than showing can sometimes be. A great and sudden feeling of distance is created in this passage, which opens a chapter, and a number of stylistic devices contribute to this. First of all there is the paragraphing: Flaubert frequently used the sentence-paragraph to heighten a statement. Proust paradoxically remarked that the blanks around the sentences were among Flaubert's finest achievements: he certainly had a feeling for paragraphing that was entirely new. The sentence structure again shows characteristic patterns: Flaubert, in his attempt to create a kind of orotund solemnity, loved to devise odd connectives or lack of them between or within sentences. Asyndeton, the omission of an *and* or *but*, is frequent, especially in enumerations; on the other hand, *and* is sometimes introduced after a semicolon, as in the last lines above, for a rhetorical flourish: it often suggests resignation and weariness.

As elaborate as the technique of *L'Education senti-mentale* is, Flaubert was not content to duplicate it, and in his last books, *Trois Contes* (1877) and the posthumous *Bouvard et Pécuchet* (1881), he explored still further possibilities in narration. "Un Coeur simple" will serve as an example. To begin with, "Un Coeur simple" has no plot in the traditional sense: neither causality nor coincidence govern its narrative fabric, which consists of an almost straight chronological exposition of a life that is indeed simple. Félicité's inarticulateness and lack of education may well have been the reason Flaubert largely abandoned not only dialogue but also the technique of free indirect discourse, which we tend to associate with him, and devised instead a peculiar narrative voice: there is far more telling than showing in "Un Coeur simple." And this voice resembles none other in Flaubert's works, because, as he said in a letter, "I want to move sensitive souls to tears, being one myself." He also specifically noted that the story is "not at all ironic" but "serious and sad."

In this new mode of narration metaphor is rare and the sentences have no oratorical cadence. Although on two or three occasions the narrator makes a brief but obtrusive comment on Félicité's intelligence, the general impression is one of a great effort toward impersonality: much use is made of short, paratactic sentences. Flaubert is determined not to direct or channel the reader's emotive response to the text; it must spring from events described in an almost neutral vocabulary. The result is a highly subtle kind of texture.

To the question "What is *Madame Bovary* about?" several plausible answers can be made; the same is not true of "Un Coeur simple." In a letter Flaubert described the story as being about "a poor country girl, pious but mystical," who "successively loves a man, her mistress' children, a nephew" and so forth. In fact, the story is far more complex than Flaubert admits. The word *mystical*, however, can serve as an initial guide into the thematics of the work. When Félicité takes Virginie to catechism class she learns of the Trinity for the first time. Of the triune god she is most impressed by his role as Holy Ghost: she immediately identifies Him with birds, fire, wind, and will-o'-the-wisps; in short, she is an instinctive pantheist, like so many of the romantic writers Flaubert had adored. There is a bit of brilliant irony in ascribing to Félicité the cult of the Holy Ghost, since His theological definition is so recondite as to be beyond the grasp of those not versed in medieval Latin (see any Catholic dictionary), and, in any case, about dogma Félicité "understood nothing."

In earlier works, *Madame Bovary* and *L'Education sentimentale*, Flaubert had used certain striking symbols of psychological emptiness and wasted time: Emma gazes out the window at dull perspectives; Frédéric watches the Seine flow by. A similiar complex of symbols is to be found in "Un Coeur simple," but they are more delicately handled. Félicité, on numerous occasions, contemplates vast spaces, empty horizons, and utter monotony. The passage where she has just learned of her nephew's death is characteristic: "Her washboard and pail lay by the edge of the Toucques. She tossed a bunch of shirts onto the bank, rolled back her sleeves, raised her clothes beater; and her scrubbing away could be heard in neighboring yards. The meadows were empty, the wind rippled the stream; at the bottom of it the tendrils of huge plants swam like a drowned man's hair." These visions of emptiness contrast with the pantheism suggested by her notion of the Holy Ghost: nature either reflects God or nothingness, and there lies the submerged irony of the story. This antithesis of a godless world and an informing Holy Ghost is brought to a kind of synthesis at the end of "Un Coeur simple" when Félicité, dying, sees an enormous paraclete-parrot soar above her.

The operation of irony in "Un Coeur simple" is rather complex; neither Félicité nor the society she lives in are the object of it. Rather, one thinks of Matthew Arnold's definition of poetry as a criticism of life. The cycle of the liturgical year lends a structure to life in Pont-L'Evêque, but the church, despite its theoretical ideas, cannot redeem the cruel laws of existence. All this, however, is merely implied: Flaubert's narrative texture remains resolutely uncommitted on the surface and completely purposeful on the level of implicitness. The avoidance of dialogue-scene and free indirect discourse is probably the most important element in elaborating so curious a fictional texture which, in many ways, violates principles of technique that Flaubert, in *Madame Bovary*, had made almost mandatory for novelists.

II

Emile Zola's early work has been carefully studied,[6] and it is obvious that his imagination differed completely from Flaubert's, although in many ways he was Flaubert's greatest disciple in matters of fictional technique and stylistic texture. Zola himself did not help serious study of his novels, because he was understandably more concerned with selling them than with getting them praised. ("I don't have a private income," he told Flaubert, who was somewhat outraged at Zola's commercial second thoughts.[7]) Decades of literary historians have taken Zola's published declarations about naturalism and truth in the novel as clues to his mind: they made of him a peculiar crank who wandered around with a notebook listening to people's chatter and noting their actions. It is true that, like Balzac and Flaubert, Zola had a passion for documentation, but it is also true that, to a greater extent than either of them, he thought out seemingly realistic novels in highly symbolic and imagistic terms. As Zola put it, "I have an overdeveloped feeling for true details, a leap from the trampoline of exact observation into the stars. Truth rises on wings to the condition of a symbol." [8] We now have all of Zola's worksheets for his novels, and we can trace the elaboration of his plots, symbols, and chapter forms.

[6] See John C. Lapp, *Zola before the "Rougon-Macquart"* (Toronto, 1964).
[7] Much interesting personal material relating to the naturalists can be found scattered through the Goncourts' *Journal*.
[8] See Philip D. Walker, *Emile Zola* (London, 1969), 10.

The naturalist (Zola privately made fun of the term himself, while finding it useful for commercial reasons) had a far more poetic imagination than Flaubert; indeed, the working out of his best novels always involved considerations of symbolism.

All of Zola's novels are worthy of some discussion, but of the earlier ones I should like to consider only *Le Ventre de Paris* (1873) and *L'Assommoir* (1877): each has a particular interest in regard to techniques; *Le Ventre de Paris* is set in Les Halles—the city market, that part of Paris which is no more and where the nightlife of the city once was centered. Zola's taste for descriptive writing was given the utmost freedom in this book, and, while sometimes it overflowed into set pieces like the "symphony of cheeses," it also showed the powerful symbolism which characterizes his best works. There is a *charcuterie* near Les Halles, and its proprietors belong to the race of the plump, as opposed to the race of the lean, represented by the proprietor's half brother. The latter had been imprisoned during the 1848 Revolution, but has escaped; Abel and Cain are clearly the archetypes here: the novel will be a struggle between brothers, and the image of it will be the conflict between leanness and "bad fat"—"la mauvaise graisse," which is an unhealthy yellow and opposed to good, pink fat. It is characteristic of Zola's lesser achievements that one of his novelistic skills—in this case symbolic description—should be preponderent, while other aspects of the work are somewhat cursorily worked out. The plot is adequate but one is left with little memory of specific scenes or cruces: the novel's plenitude is one of edibles rather than incident. *L'Assommoir*, on the other hand, is an experiment in a purely fictional problem: the devising of a new kind of narrating voice.

One of the problems Flaubert faced in writing *Madame Bovary* was the disparity between the author's highly literary voice and a style for indirect discourse which would seem suitable for Emma's banal emotions. He found a kind of shifting compromise: here and there Emma thinks in the style of books she has read; elsewhere her words are quoted directly. This is all very well when dealing with a young woman who "reads too much," but these ambiguities are impossible with a very literate author treating the character of an almost illiterate washerwoman, such as Gervaise in *L'Assommoir*. Zola took the plunge and devised a narrative tone which one still encounters today. His notion was to blend together description, indirect discourse, and dialogue into a stylistic continuum where the grammar and vocabulary must fuse so that the reader feels no disparity among them. This stylistic formula completely shocked Flaubert: he called it "inverted preciosity," because the narrator's voice is discreetly colored with slang and lower-class usage. There is consequently a good deal of ambiguity; at times it is difficult to distinguish between the narrator and free indirect discourse on the part of the characters. Here are Copeau's plans for the wedding: "In the meantime Copeau didn't have a dime. Without trying to show off, he intended to do things right. . . . Sure, he didn't like the skirts, it killed him to pay his six bucks to those fat pigs who didn't need it to wet their whistles. But a wedding without a mass, whatever you say, it's just not a wedding. He went himself to the church to bargain and for an hour hassled with a dirty old crow who would have sold his own grandmother." Zola can occasionally, with some attention to transition, rise to a more formal tone, but this tends to be reserved for solemn moments.

L'Assommoir was Zola's first great success, and, with his usual foxy sense of publicity, he planned his subsequent novels (a general scheme for them already existed) so that, rather than following any strict chronological order in the history of the Rougon-Macquarts, they varied in genre and tone. This arrangement had the advantage of regularly surprising the reading public, and avoiding the monotonous character of a true *roman-fleuve*. (Actually many little changes were made in the temporal relations of the various plots, so that the conception of the whole grew over the years; Zola was not following some dry plan.) *L'Assommoir*, for example, was followed by *Une Page d'amour*, which, in turn, preceded a return to really sordid topics in *Nana*. Likewise the novels are involved to widely varying degrees in social and political questions. The use of symbolism also changes greatly from book to book. Aside from Zola's unfortunate tendency to crudely personify machines, we find that certain works have elaborate patterns of imagery which are not to be found in others. Nor does the taste for symbolism exclude highly committed social themes and attitudes, despite the silly antithesis so commonly made between realist and symbolist modes. Both currents reach perhaps their highest point in *Germinal* (1885), which, in addition, offers us the most elaborate example of Zola's devising new and significant handlings of the correlation of time and point of view.

The first two of the seven parts of *Germinal* recount the events of one long day, but not at all in the manner of Balzac. Zola created a curious and subtle shifting back and forth between hours and characters. The novel begins with Etienne's arrival before dawn at the mine in search of work. The second chapter describes the awakening and departure of the working members of the

Maheu family. From Chapter 3 on, we are again following Etienne's consciousness as he sees the Maheus arrive at the mine, is employed, learns through the day the
routine of his job, and leaves in the afternoon with
Maheu, who finds him lodgings. Part II now returns us
to eight o'clock in the morning and the awakening of
the Grégoire family. We see their typical preoccupations
until the moment when la Maheude arrives to ask for
help. This conclusion of the first chapter serves as a
liaison to the next one, which moves us again back in
time to the hours between the working Maheus' departure and la Maheude's getting herself together and
setting off for the Grégoires'. We now move through
the whole scene of la Maheude at the Grégoires' and
follow her day through to five o'clock in the afternoon:
we meet her neighbors, Maheu comes home, having left
Etienne at the end of Part I, and they busily eat, bathe,
make love, and garden. Part II concludes with Etienne's
activities from twilight to nine o'clock.

All this elaborate backtracking in time and shifting
from one consciousness to another demonstrates a stage
of virtuosity well beyond anything Flaubert ever dreamed
of and anticipates certain devices in *Ulysses*. What is
particularly skillful is the way in which chapters do not
necessarily regress to the point in time which another
has begun; they tend more to overlap partially, with the
exact moment of the day often suggested rather than
precisely indicated. It sometimes happens with this technique that a scene occurs twice or more in the narrative,
as point of view shifts from chapter to chapter. In Part
IV, for example, we first hear at the luncheon party
that a delegation of miners has arrived to present their
grievances. In the following chapter we see the miners

going to press their case. A far more dramatic example occurs in Part V, where in Chapter 2 those in the Jean-Bart mine learn that the cables of the elevator have been cut; in the next chapter, Zola redoes it all as seen by the hostile mob on the surface. And finally, in Chapter 5 of the same part, Zola actually indicates the hour—five o'clock—three times as the scene and point of view shift from one group of characters to another. The high sophistication by which the chapters and parts of *Germinal* are interwoven introduces a new kind of illusionism into realist fiction: once the simple, smooth line of chronology is broken, it is possible to imagine all manner of peculiar effects, including some of more recent invention.

Equally striking in *Germinal* is the cosmology of the novel, with its numerous allusions to myth. Of all Zola's novels this is the one in which symbol prevails most over conventional notions of realism or, more accurately, is blended with them. I do not think that cosmology is too pretentious a word for Zola's representations of the moon, the sun, the surface of the earth and its bowels, and, finally, the cycle of the ages.[9]

At first we see the plain alternately sterile and fecund; the idea of a crop, present in the title *Germinal*, is supported by many references to harvest, but the harvest will be one of men: the agricultural cycle is primarily symbolic of social change, and the sun figuratively presides over this, both the mild April sun, as at the end of the book, and the red winter sun bathing the landscape in blood, as the mob of striking miners rushes over the plain: "And what they [the bourgeois] saw was a red

[9] See Philip D. Walker, "Prophetic Myths in Zola," *PMLA*, lxxiv (1959), 444-52.

vision of the revolution that would inevitably carry
them all off one bloody evening at the end of this epoch.
. . . Fires would blaze . . . not a single stone would be
left standing in the cities, and men would return to
primitive life in the woods after the great orgy."

The red sun, of course, suggests another complex of
myth and color symbolism: during Etienne's first day in
the mine, red and black, the colors of hell, are constantly
mentioned, although Zola, with his description of water
pouring into the pit, is preparing us for the ultimate
symbol of the mine—the uncharted subterranean sea,
which the sabotaged mine will become. Another form
of infernal symbolism is Le Tartaret (from a Greek
word for Hell), the mine which has been burning for
years and so warms the ground that there is vegetation
all year round. It is interesting that Mme Hennebeau
and her party, on the day violence breaks forth, go to
see this as a curiosity: they admire it without remember-
ing the loss of life which it caused. For Catherine, working in the nearby Jean-Bart, Le Tartaret is a punishment
visited on the mine crew for their sins. Various other
elements of the supernatural are associated with the
Voreux mine: the Black Man who comes to punish loose
female mine workers, the yellow horses Etienne sees as
he first approaches the mine (horses are never yellow
in French or English: this is a fantastic beast), and the
red cat who leaps from the mine just before it collapses
(needless to say, cats are never red). The collapse of
the superstructure of the mine again brings in a myth:
it is compared to a giant, that is, to one of the Titans
whom Zeus hurled into Hades.

A special group of associations is found in passages
dealing with the Grégoire family. Their colors are white,
pink, and blue, their estate a garden of Eden, a protected

orchard in the dismal plain.[10] But the enjoyment of all this is only possible by their worship of the "hidden god," who manifests himself through stock in a corporation—felicitously called in French an Anonymous Society. The Grégoires constitute the perfect antithesis to the miners, which is why their house and attitudes are so carefully portrayed. The other principal bourgeois in the novel are too caught up in personal problems to really serve as a foil in the depiction of the two classes.

A discussion in real detail of symbolism in *Germinal* could be very lengthy and certain points might remain moot; for example, is the moon, which is mentioned so often during the miners' nighttime meeting, intended to be sinister, or is it merely a structural device, a unifying element in the chapter? Rather than attempt to solve such a question it is here more relevant to suggest the general relations between Zola's work at its best and the kind of novels which other writers were publishing under the influence of Flaubert and Edmond de Goncourt.

III

Maupassant's fiction was supposedly modeled after that of Flaubert, who gave him lessons in the art of prose narration. Some of Maupassant's short stories have survived as neat examples of the genre, but most are not likely to attract readers among those interested in fictional technique. The reason for this—and it is far more true of his novels—is that Maupassant was completely indifferent to the great range of the French language; he might do a good job of peasant speech now and then,

10 See Philip D. Walker, "Zola's Use of Color Imagery in *Germinal*," *PMLA*, lxxvii (1962), 442–49.

but he had no sense of how to heighten a passage, no ear for grand rhythms, and hopeless vulgarity in his choice of images. He ridiculed those who worked seriously on problems of style, whereas he would write lines like "she looked like an angel." One wonders what went wrong in Flaubert's teaching; *le mot juste*, supposedly for reasons of clarity, became *le mot banal*.

A very characteristic novel of the period is *Une Belle Journée* (1881) by Henry Céard. This medium-length work describes, for the most part, a long, dull day spent in a private room of a restaurant by a self-styled ladies' man and a neighbor's wife, prudish and equally dreary, who has foolishly, almost against her will, consented to meet him on a Sunday when her husband is out of town. It is evident from the very beginning that nothing will come of it: the title is ironic, since cool weather prevents them from going to the countryside and a storm forces them to remain indoors together. The novel was famous in its day and much damned, as well as praised, for carrying to an extreme the example of negative plot provided by *L'Education sentimentale*. Many stylistic devices of the later Flaubert are present such as abundant free indirect discourse, elaborate attempts to vary sentence structures, and a preference for long, heavy adverbs. A book like this has primarily historical interest, but it contains remarkable invention of detail, indispensable in so protracted an essentially dull episode, and the detail involves not only conversations between people who barely know each other, but also their varying feelings in the course of the hours.

Our last example of objective narration is a most peculiar and significant one: *Sous-offs* (1889) by Lucien Descaves. Descaves usually can be found in literary histories as one of "the five" who published a manifesto (1887) against Zola's *La Terre* (1886), condemning the utter filth of the book. It has been recently suggested that Zola, with his usual instinct for publicity, put "the five" up to it, and the fact that *Sous-offs* was later put on trial for its obscene and insulting descriptions of life in the peacetime French army would seem to confirm that Descaves was no *belle âme*. The interesting thing, however, about *Sous-offs* is not whether Descaves had bested Zola in foulness, but the peculiar stylistic medium through which he renders the stench and ordure of barracks life. Descaves was a disciple of Edmond de Goncourt in matters of language; that is, he admired the later Goncourt style, which rivals the most bizarre inventions of the younger symbolist poets. Here is a characteristic passage (which it is impossible to render into English): "C'était, d'abord, la Porte de Vanves, évoquant une rumeur de marché, le piétonnement moutonnier des recrues, vaguant sous la pourriture d'un ciel, dont les violets gangréneux, en dépit de copieuses ponctions, publiaient la décomposition hivernale." Outside of satire, parody, or pastiche, where the device is common, it is quite exceptional to find such disparity between level of style and subject matter. The syntax and vocabulary are, to say the least, high-flown and even esoteric, whereas the subject could not be more down-to-earth. This is an extreme example of a tendency—deeply rooted and often ignored—in the French realist-naturalist movement, to present banal or debased characters and actions in a style which we would not associate with them, as if rhetorical devices could transform mud into gems.

The paradox of the stylistically recherché treatment of the quotidian arose with Flaubert and his worry over writing "Chateaubrianized Balzac." Flaubert clearly saw that with his ideal of prose diction and rhythm, suggested in part by Chateaubriand's confession novels, he risked a considerable chance of mismatching words and actions. However his choice of *grands liseurs* for his central characters in *Madame Bovary* and *L'Education sentimentale* makes his elaborate style plausible, and the hollow solemnity of his rhythms seems almost to echo the emptiness of his characters' hearts, while generous quotations of banalities suggest the reality of their minds. Flaubert's working out of the problem could not do, however, for a book like *L'Assommoir* dealing with the proletariat, and Zola, therefore, was obliged to find his own linguistic level, which involved, among other things, giving the narrating voice something of the flavor of the characters' speech. On the other hand, the Goncourts' novels, and especially those written by Edmond alone (see above all *La Fille Elisa* [1877], his first venture into the novel after his brother's death), are quite devoid of plot interest or striking realistic detail, and seem hardly to exist but as vehicles for a curiously contorted style. In sum, the whole realist-naturalist movement is significant not only for the milieus and manners presented, but also as an attempt to create new narrative effects and stylistic surfaces. *L'Assommoir* and *La Fille Elisa* are at opposite poles: in the former, narrator and milieu fuse, in the latter the prose is not in the least congruent with the subject matter but tries to carry the subject through a supposedly heightening rhetoric. Flaubert's choice of subject relieved him of solving this dilemma and made of him a model for numerous lesser novelists, like Céard, who were content to explore the bourgeois world with the tools of the master. But the problems raised by objective narration were such that a reaction against it occurred in the decades after Flaubert's death; and that is what we now must examine.

5

Beyond Impersonal Narration

FLAUBERT'S IDEAL OF OBJECTIVE NARRATION and the concealed narrator helps define the dominant formal characteristics of much of French fiction in the second half of the nineteenth century. However, the notion of impersonal fiction was no sooner established than it began to break up.[1] New forms of narrative arose, in which sometimes the element of plot molds the structure less than before. In the naturalist period proper, two important works illustrate this emergent tendency in the novel: *A rebours* and *Les Lauriers sont coupés.*

In Joris-Karl Huysmans' career as a writer, *A rebours* (1884) had been preceded by naturalist tales such as *Marthe,* the story of a prostitute, almost an inevitable subject, which Edmond de Goncourt, Daudet, and Zola also tried their hand at. Like Goncourt, and unlike Zola, Huysmans had little imagination for plot structure: all his efforts went into his elaborate style with its archaisms, neologisms, and generally rare words. These were not to find their full power until a suitable subject matter

---

[1] See Michel Raimond, *La Crise du roman: Des Lendemains du naturalisme aux années vingt* (Paris, 1968).

came to hand: *A rebours* is a peculiar bridge between the novel and the attitudinizings of contemporary "decadent" poets. The book is probably the first after *Mademoiselle de Maupin* whose subject is taste and estheticism, but unlike Gautier's work, which is a confession novel, and unlike the customary naturalist one, *A rebours* is an example of an encyclopedic form of narration. The chapters deal with the main character's hobbies, like collecting fine books, strange flowers, or odd liqueurs; a few of them contain episodes such as the trip to England, that never proceeds beyond an English-style pub near the Gare Saint-Lazare, in which Des Esseintes feels so strong a British atmosphere that he dares not spoil it by crossing the channel, but, for the most part, the chapters are essay-prose-poems on late Latin literature, symbolist verse, or similar "decadent" subjects. For *A rebours* is a handbook, a treatise on decadence, as it was understood in esthetic terms toward the end of the nineteenth century. A good number of Zola's novels are, of course, encyclopedic in that they convey vast amounts of quite specialized information about Les Halles, mines, laundries, farming, or the railway, but plot is always used to mitigate or disguise this function of the novel. Huysmans' very arrangement of topics in *A rebours* draws attention to a strong authorial presence. Yet technically, in chapter structure, stylistic polish, and consistent handling of point of view, *A rebours* remains very much in the realist-naturalist tradition, while absorbing material we associate with poetry. The "lyrical novel" was to find favor in the early twentieth century—Colette, for example, comes to mind—and *A rebours* is, along with *Mademoiselle de Maupin*, one of its ancestors. Huysmans' later works such as *Là-bas*, a study in Satanism, or *La Cathédrale*, dealing with Chartres, abandon more and more the conventions of fiction for the essay form.

Edouard Dujardin, on the other hand, devised, for *Les Lauriers sont coupés* (1888), a more startling and more exclusively narrative innovation. He invented a form of interior monologue (a French term synonymous with stream-of-consciousness which I shall use except when I wish to suggest the syntactic disorder of Joyce). This device, in its radical form, was completely ignored until Joyce drew attention to it and acknowledged his indebtedness to it for *Ulysses*. At the same time, one must add that Dujardin's book embodies a merely potentially great technique; he did not realize it fully, and since his story is insignificant both in plot and resonance, it is not altogether surprising that his ultimate fame came only as a reflection of Joyce's.

Dujardin's *monologue intérieur* is a matter of both syntax and content. In regard to grammar, the dominant tense and sentence pattern are present and paratactic; sentence fragments, largely nouns and adjectives, abound, as well as imperatives, exclamations (*pourquoi, bonjour*), and other simple elements of communication. Jerky rhythms, three closed periods indicating the drifting off of consciousness, and abrupt colons and semi-colons (He:followed by discourse) characterize the typographical rendering of mental activity, and only an occasional arty inversion of subject, verb, and predicate adjective reminds us, in the revised 1925 version, that this is a book written under the sway of symbolist ideas on style.

The content is characterized by a fusion of inner thought and exterior action; this is the most important discovery on the way to *Ulysses*:

At least in a restaurant you're not bored. What's that waiter up to? He's coming. He's bringing the sole. Funny things soles. About four mouthfuls in this one and there are others that could make a meal for ten people; of course they stretch it out with sauce. Well, let's get at

it; a shrimp and mussel sauce would be a distinct im-
provement. That time we went shrimping in the ocean;
not much of a catch, it added up to nothing and my feet
were sopping wet even though I was wearing those heavy
tan shoes I bought near the Stock Exchange. What an
endless business picking away at fish; I'm not getting any-
where! I must owe a hundred francs, more, to my boot-
maker. I might try to learn something about stocks and
bonds on the market; that would be a sound idea. I could
never figure out what they meant by speculating for a
fall . . . .

The simplistic sentence structure and lack of logical
order are an attempt to capture the reality of the mind's
life, in which nothing is detached from circumstances.
Dujardin, like Joyce after him, believed there was a
pre-linguistic form of thought which could only be
represented by the plainest of constructions. The result
is the utter opposite of Flaubert's refining vulgar life
into noble cadences. Yet there is some connection, theoretically at least, between Flaubert's free indirect discourse and stream-of-consciousness writing: both seek
to render inner life. However, Flaubert conceived of
language in a traditional, esthetic way; Dujardin used it
as if he believed that important truths of psychology
could be communicated through his idiosyncratic style,
and the dream which occurs toward the end of *Les
Lauriers sont coupés* represents a kind of experience
which Flaubert's techniques were incapable of rendering:

She is asleep. I'm nearly asleep myself, my eyes half-
closed . . . this is her body; the rise and fall of her
breast, her blended fragrance . . . . the room, high fire-
place . . . the dining room . . . my father . . . sitting
together, we three . . . . you, you alone of all beloved,
from the beginning, Antonia . . . glitter of lights everywhere . . . are you laughing? . . . lines of streetlamps

stretching out to infinity . . . night . . . cold, icy night
. . . . the room . . . Léa . . . . Good Lord, was I
dreaming?

Other incidents, such as a question of personal hygiene
when Daniel thinks Léa will keep him for the night,
would have been far too low for Flaubert's consideration.

One very interesting question remains: how, by using
monologue intérieur, does Dujardin create the ironic
tone of his novel? Theoretically the stream-of-consciousness technique should place us so completely within the
principal character that we should feel only *with* him
and never against him. (Virginia Woolf regularly accomplished this.) Here, however, it is not the case, and
we must resort to the notion of the unreliable narrator—
a device we shall encounter more and more frequently
—to explain the tone of the novel. The reader sees,
through the mere presentation of telltale facts, that Léa
is a classic golddigger and that Daniel Prince is a rather
wishy-washy and very romantic young man. In short,
the narrative is based on implication, more so even than
"Un Coeur simple," and on the reader's ability to see
what is false or foolish in the characters. If the reader
is inadequate, the story will seem senseless or wrong-
headed; if he shares the author's implied view, it will be
transparent. But we have, in any case, reached the complete opposite of the commented-on story. Not a single
word comes from an author's voice identifiable as such.
We must judge Daniel Prince against our own mental
divagations and excursus.

One last point remains, and one which relates the
novel especially to *Ulysses:* the whole action (dedicated
to Racine and his tight interpretation of the twenty-
four hour unity) takes place between about six o'clock

and midnight on an evening in April 1887. The time it takes to read the novel with care corresponds roughly to the unfolding of its action: as in Racine's *Bérénice*, reality and convention miraculously coincide.

The subsequent fate of interior monologue transcends the history of French fiction while remaining part of it. Joyce, especially in the third chapter of *Ulysses*, relieved the monotony of Dujardin's first-person, present-tense monologue by interspersing third-person, past-tense indications of movement and gesture. In "Mon Plus Secret Conseil" (1920), Valéry Larbaud followed Joyce's pattern, while mingling in free indirect discourse. But the most complicated refinement Joyce introduced was the mixture of sentence fragments, run-on syntax, and word deformations, devices which for rhythmic reasons are difficult to adapt to French. (An exception: Eugène Ionesco has done marvelous Joyced words in his plays.)

The occasional interior monologues in important novels of the twenties—one can be found, from time to time, in Proust or Gide—do not add up to much, but in *La Nausée*, Sartre attempted at one point, despite the diary form of the novel, a genuinely Joycean stream-of-consciousness pattern with alliterations and mixed-up syntax of various kinds. Finally, the New Novelists of the fifties, partly perhaps under the influence of Faulkner, reintroduced forms of stream-of-consciousness into the French novel which make little attempt to imitate the more idiosyncratic manner of Joyce.

In 1886, when Zola was nearing the end of the Rougon-Macquart cycle, an event occurred which was to alter considerably French conceptions of the novel: Eugène-Melchior de Vogüé's essays on the Russian novel were published in book form and inspired publishers to bring out translations of whatever Russian fiction they could discover.[2] Vogüé's bias in his criticism is scarcely concealed: as a conservative and a Catholic he was determined to show that there existed a form of literary realism far superior to Zola's, in that it took account of man's spiritual life. His ideas became immediately fashionable, and, in the literary conversation that opens Huysmans' *Là-bas* (1891), we find a characteristic discussion of a "spiritual Naturalism" that would be parallel and complementary to Zola's; Dostoievsky is inevitably mentioned as the writer who most approximates this ideal of fiction.

Of the great Russian novelists, Dostoievsky was the strangest and by far the most influential on important French writers. In a sense there is a kind of hidden logic to this: Dostoievsky himself had been heavily influenced by Balzac, and French translations of his novels seem, in style and technique, to resemble *La Comédie humaine* more than anything else. Obviously the thematics are quite different on the surface, but certain profound connections have been traced.[3] It is curious that Dostoievsky and Flaubert were almost exact contemporaries; both were, in one way or another, deeply indebted to Balzac, and Flaubert's influence on the French novel partially ended—at least insofar as impersonal narration is concerned—just at the moment when the reading public discovered Dostoievsky's novels with their old-fashioned authorial intrusions and their penchant for including serious ideological discussions, much as Balzac had done some decades before. It is as if the French novel were

[2] See F. W. Hemmings, *The Russian Novel in France: 1884–1914* (London, 1950).

[3] See Joel Hunt, "Balzac and Dostoevskij: Ethics and Eschatology," *Slavic and East European Journal*, XVI (1958), 307–24.

being rejuvenated by something it had once achieved and subsequently lost, only to regain it through a foreign intermediary.

It is not easy to state categorically that this or that French novel was marked by Russian influence, but it is perfectly clear that after 1886 the novel tends to revert to authorial interventions, discussions of ideas, and generous use of the first person, often through the means of a diary or letters. In short, some rather old techniques are being revived, but only after a period when matters of style were felt to be all-important and which transformed the novelist's attitude toward the surface of his prose. As one might expect, some less gifted novelists like Paul Bourget and Maurice Barrès—both quite famous in their day—fabricated dreary "novels of ideas" in what passed for elegant style, but we shall sidestep them in order to examine works by Charles-Louis Philippe, André Gide, Alain-Fournier, and François Mauriac.

Bubu-de-Montparnasse (1901) is Charles-Louis Philippe's masterpiece, and it is quite obvious that the Russian novelists' concern with evangelical thought had deeply influenced his socialist ideas. The plot, slow to get started and relatively simple, deals with a young and poor provincial in Paris, Pierre Hardy, a prostitute, Berthe, whom he meets and tries to redeem, and the return from prison of her pimp, Bubu, who drags her once again into the street. A friend of Pierre's, Louis Buisson, comments from time to time on events in a tone quite reminiscent of *Crime and Punishment:* "You have to love pitiful whores. I've always believed that if we couldn't save them, it's because we can't love them enough." Later he speaks of studying the Gospels.

Alongside the thematic inspiration derived from the Russians, however, we recognize definite post-Flaubertian techniques, which would not have existed save for the master of Croisset. Free indirect discourse is common in this novel, and occasional paragraphs have the laconic, elliptic quality which Flaubert so prized in his later years: "Little Berthe one evening left her father's house to go live with Maurice. Her sister Marthe was pregnant at that time. The kid, Blanche, had stolen five francs from her boss." However, despite the abundance of passages employing Flaubert's characteristic techniques, the novel strikes one above all as being anti-Flaubertian, and very distinctive in its authorial voice. As the book opens we are aware of an author who seems quite familiar with the milieu of his pimps and whores. "The whores were about their business. There's la petite Gabrielle, who lived for two years with Robert, the one who murdered Constance. Her lover has just left, sentenced to hard labor. There's little Jeanne, who's probably about sixteen. Since last month she's been working the boulevard Sébastopol." Elsewhere he occasionally comments, or fuses with character and reader, as in the description of Louis Buisson's room: "The window opened onto a big river channel, toward the Pont-Neuf and its little park . . . Are we in Paris? We're high in the air, in a fluvial country. . . ." Second-person sentences can be directed to the characters, the reader, or to God. Here Bubu-Maurice is burglarizing: "They went at it with dry throats and itchy hands. Go on, all three of you, my brothers, make your hearts skip a beat and see what you can in burglaries, when you shake, hunt, and find." This reflection about Berthe's life draws the reader into the narrative fabric: "Now Berthe was a prostitute. That's not a job you can leave at dawn and, away from it, be yourself like some clerk outside the office. Do you know how vice smells once you've sniffed it . . . ?" And finally there is the meditation addressed to God: "It's nothing, Lord. Just a woman on the street, walking and earning her living because it's hard to do anything else. A man stops and speaks to her because you gave us women for pleasure. And then this woman is Berthe, and well, you know the rest. It's nothing."

Much use is also made of the ambiguous French pronoun *on*, which, especially in familiar speech, can refer indiscriminately to first, second, or third persons, singular or plural. On one occasion tenses and persons are jumbled together (Maurice-Bubu is drunk, which justifies this peculiar effect): "He passed in front of the big grocery . . . and saw boxes of tangerines. Little tangerines, little juicy nothings, you're not made for a pimp's stomach. . . . You think it's hard; you have to judge with your eye; no one's looking. You have to grab it, quick and coolly." Philippe's use of persons and tenses seems, at first, anarchic: they obey no familiar grammatical logic, and suggest, with their *I, we, you, they, he,* shifts of perspective, a chaotic mode of narration; however, instead of chaos, we discover, on close examination, subtle forms of transition between points of view, which are made all the more effective by discreet patterns of punctuation: dialogue and apostrophe are frequently not distinguished, or hardly distinguished typographically from the narrating voice.

But we have yet to examine the strangest uses of authorial intervention in the novel. The first one occurs when the narrator quotes a line of Lamartine known to all educated Frenchmen but hardly to Berthe: "Now everything swirled around her: Paris, the hospital, the present, the future, and vague emotions: 'Un seul être

vous manque et tout est dépeuplé.' " Later on an eloquent sermon is followed by a disclaimer: "No, he who
is your spouse is a man, and all flesh, suffering flesh and
struggling soul must be dearer to our hearts than any
desire, any hatred. . . . Bow thy head beneath God's
justice like a good angel; then look up and smile upon
Satan, your brother. . . . That's not the way Pierre
spoke; that's not the way Berthe understood him, but
these words charged the air in the room and passed over
them, as if they were a higher version of their human
speech." There is no theoretic precedent for such odd
narration in the late nineteenth-century conception of
the novel.

Actually, the seemingly chaotic details we have pointed
out in *Bubu* coalesce beautifully: the narrative voice is
not rigidly subdivided into author, character, or author
addressing himself to reader behind his characters' back.
A very smooth continuum allows all of us—author,
character, and reader—to move gently from one center
of consciousness to another: the novel is an extraordinarily delicate blend of several techniques into a pleasing
whole.

Bubu-de-Montparnasse has one other remarkable fictional pattern which I have postponed discussing and
which probably is the most powerful element in the
book's hold on the reader: the language of causality
which is so prominent in the narrative.[4] Clauses and
phrases beginning with *because, since,* and *because of*
are strangely intrusive in *Bubu-de-Montparnasse*. In fact,
it often happens that *because* (*parce que* or *puisque*) is
repeated in the same sentence whereas correct written
French would demand merely *parce que/puisque* . . .

---

[4] See Leo Spitzer, *Linguistics and Literary History: Essays in
Stylistics* (New York, 1962), 11–14.

et que. Spitzer concludes that Philippe constantly violates the usual principles of usage in order to obtain a
massive, inexorable feeling of fatality. Here is an example of this: "Maurice's friends didn't work much because their women worked for them and because they
knew the world well enough they didn't need to work.
She saw pimps and pickpockets in everyday life, and
realized that they didn't want to work because doing
what you wish to is more fun." The dark logic of the
novel evolves thus: "He became a pimp because he lived
in a society full of rich men, who are powerful and determine your career. They want women for their money.
There certainly have to be pimps to supply them." On
the client's side the same determinism obtains: "Since we
live in a world where pleasures cost money, Pierre calculated that this particular pleasure was worth five francs."
This ferocious logic was Voltaire's invention, and no
novelist in the ensuing decades before Charles-Louis
Philippe, Stendhal excepted, understood the devastating
effect of this rhetoric. A kind of insane, dark concatena-
tion of *because* and *therefore*, *since*, and *one needs*, *because of*, and *thus* leads us on in the nightmare of Pierre,
Berthe, and Maurice: only an absolute moral principle
like that of the Gospels can release them; only the spell
cast by Dostoievsky at the end of *Crime and Punishment*, when redemption holds forth its promise, can res-
cue them from the fate of *because* and *since*. We have
come a long way from the peaceful and pessimistic determinism of "Un Coeur simple." Flaubert was completely involved in suffering—human and animal—but
saw no redemption. Moreover he had no use for ideological polemic in the novel: he felt the intrusion of ideas
as such would mar its artistry and accomplish nothing.

And this, perhaps, separates him more than anything from his successors.

The peculiar point of view in *Bubu-de-Montparnasse* comes from a kind of conflation of the traditional categories of author, character, and reader. Another quite original medium of narration is that devised by Alain-Fournier (the pseudonym of Henri-Alban Fournier) for *Le Grand Meaulnes* (1913). *Meaulnes* is a first-person novel, but totally unlike those of the romantic period: the story is told, not by the central character but by a secondary one, who, moreover, does not understand the inner life of the protagonist. This means that we must read the novel with a kind of mistrust of the narrator and with an effort to fathom, through the facts the narrator provides, the real meaning of the action.

In Part I, François tells us, in chapters carefully related to weather, sharpened with vivid final sentences, and occasionally cast in a present-tense *monologue intérieur*, about Meaulnes' settling into the Seurel family's life, his "adventure" in the "secret domain," and the account of it he gives François. So far the narrative is remarkable for its pristinely innocent quality, its mysterious geography, a wonderful use of sea imagery coupled with winter landscapes, and the phantasmagoria of the strange party, with its tersely presented side plot of Frantz's losing his fiancée.

The second part of *Le Grand Meaulnes* consists of a gradual transition from François and Meaulnes as boys to their adulthood. At the beginning, François and Meaulnes have lost all their friends because of jealousy over Meaulnes' adventure. This leads to all sorts of war games of a distinctly puerile nature, which are kept

hidden from adults, and to the mysterious appearance of
Frantz as the gypsy's assistant. It is important to observe here what François cannot see: that Meaulnes
could, of course, if he wished, easily identify Frantz,
but that would destroy the illusion he is building around
himself and the aura of mystery which is essential to his
private vision. Meaulnes does not want the Domain to
be rediscovered, for that would destroy the wholeness,
the specialness of his experience there. Meaulnes is playing an elaborate game—very suited to a wary adolescent
—in which everyone must be deceived in order that he
triumph and keep intact this richest episode in his life.

When the false spring comes and the schoolboys
play hooky, François has an experience which is central
to the thematics of the novel, although he does not know
it. He leaves his father as they enter the wood searching
for the other boys:

> Taking a shortcut I soon reached the edge of the wood,
> walking through the countryside quite alone for the
> first time in my life, like a scout who has lost touch with
> his corporal.
>   It seems to me that I must be very close to that myste-
> rious state of perfect happiness that Meaulnes caught a
> brief glimpse of one day. I have the whole morning to
> myself, free to explore the edge of the woods, the most
> remote and untrodden part of all the surrounding coun-
> tryside, while my friend and brother is exploring else-
> where.

The present tense conveys the vivid unfolding of a mysterious state like that we find in Rimbaud's prose-poems.
François is moving toward a mythic and timeless place,
where a revelation awaits him:

> For the first time in my life I too have embarked on
> an adventure. This time I am not merely out with Mon-
> sieur Seurel looking for shells left by the tide or orchis that

the schoolmaster himself cannot identify; I am not even
looking, as we often did, for that hidden spring in old Martin's field, covered with a grating and so overgrown with
weeds that it took us longer to find it each time... No,
I am looking for something even more elusive: the secret
passage of the fairy-tale, the ancient pathway choked
with thorns which the exhausted prince seeks in vain.

It appears at the most unexpected moment when you
have long forgotten that it will soon be eleven o'clock,
noon... Suddenly in the thickest part of the underbrush you hesitantly raise your hands to push aside the
branches on either side of your face, and catch sight of
a long dark avenue ending in a tiny round speck of light.

This is perhaps the height of the book's poetry, and it
dissolves suddenly into ordinary reality—a warning
which François does not heed and which foreshadows
the whole ultimate development of the plot:

But in the midst of these tantalizing dreams I suddenly
emerge into a sort of clearing which turns out to be
nothing more than a meadow. Without realizing it, I
have reached the end of the woods which I had always
imagined infinitely far away. There on my right is the
game warden's . . . . In previous years when we reached
the entrance to the woods, we always used to point to
the speck of light at the far end of the vast black avenue
and say: "That's the game warden's lodge down there,
Baladier's place." But we had never been that far. We
sometimes heard people say: "He's been all the way to
the game warden's!..." as if it were a fantastic achievement.

This time I went all the way to Baladier's lodge and
found nothing.

The childhood fantasy is exploded, and mythic dimensions are reduced to everyday geography. In other
words, François' adventure is, in its beginning, a kind
of miniature version of Meaulnes', but, unlike Meaulnes',
it is carried to a practical, logical conclusion which does

away with any mystery attached earlier to it. However François learns nothing from this, and the rest of the novel will be based on his well-intentioned confusion between the state of mind which is Meaulnes' and a reality which he assumes determines it.

After Meaulnes' precipitous departure from Sainte-Agathe (how odd to go look for Yvonne in Paris) comes a crucial chapter entitled "I betray our secret," in which François, Jasmin Delouche (the onomastics of the novel are perfect), and other village boys clandestinely drink liqueurs as François tells them of Meaulnes' "secret": the visit to the lost domain. But what was a secret for schoolboys no longer is for adolescents:

> Is it because I do not tell the story well? It certainly does not produce the effect I expected.
> It takes more than this to impress my companions, true country boys who are not easily surprised.
> "It was a wedding, what of it?" says Boujardon.
> Delouche has seen one at Préveranges that was far more extraordinary.
> The manor? There must be people in the neighborhood who have heard of it.
> The girl? Meaulnes will marry her when he has done his year's military service.

This is the point of view of boys who are too old to make up secret maps: they know accurate maps can be procured in a shop and that, in any case, by asking around among adults they can discover whatever they want to know about the region.

Meaulnes had carefully avoided asking adults about the domain, and it never occurs to François to wonder why; he is not only an unreliable narrator of his story but often a very naïve one. This shows up in the chapter called "Meaulnes' Three Letters." Meaulnes provides some information about the Galais family and Frantz's fiancée, but he also asks to be forgotten, which is the last thing the practical, meddling François is likely to do. When Meaulnes writes: "Perhaps when we die, death alone will provide the key, the sequel and the ending to this abortive adventure," François does not understand that Meaulnes sees his adventure in metaphysical terms, not merely as a matter of secret maps (those are designed to throw off François). An intellectually acute commentator on *Le Grand Meaulnes* insists on the difference between a secret, such as the location of the "lost domain," and which can be solved, and a mystery, which, by definition, cannot be explained away.[5] Meaulnes conceives of his adventure as a mystery while for François it is merely a secret, and he proceeds to treat it as such. Meaulnes baffles François when the latter comes to tell him that Yvonne has been found and the Lost Domain identified. Meaulnes had been on the verge of traveling in search of Frantz, continuing, in his mind, his initial adventure; François makes him, rather against his will, meet and marry Yvonne. The third part of the novel consists of a conflict between François' ideal of happiness (a favorite word of his) and Meaulnes' penchant for adventure. The final mishap, the hopeless marriage of Yvonne and Meaulnes, comes from the latter's yielding to François' persuasion and temporarily suppressing his native instincts. The last word of the novel is, appropriately, *adventure*, as François imagines Meaulnes departing again with his infant daughter.

The contrasts between happiness and adventure, between the possibility of recapturing the past—as François had tried to do by recreating the strange party in the Lost Domain down to reproducing the guest list—

[5] Robert Champigny, *Portrait of a Symbolist Hero* (Bloomington, 1954), see especially 109–24.

and realizing that the past can never be reborn, provides the dialectic articulation of the concluding chapters of *Le Grand Meaulnes*. In order to render this metaphysical theme within the framework of an essentially realistic narrative, Fournier allows it to be only partially perceived by his narrator, but clearly deducible by the attentive reader. François has, at the end, some inkling of how enigmatic destinies are being fulfilled with Frantz and Valentine's return to the Domain and with Meaulnes' impending redeparture, yet the mystery of Meaulnes' inner life still eludes him, as it must also, to some extent, the reader.

Two other kinds of deceptive narrators occur in well-known novels by André Gide, for the possibilities in deception—of oneself or others, in good faith or with unconscious hostility—are extremely broad. The more puzzling one tells his own story in *L'Immoraliste* (1902). He deals with a period of bad health following an excess of scholarly work, during which, at the point of greatest despair, he becomes converted to life, sunshine, and sensuality. (The turn-of-the-century hedonism of the book is sometimes embarrassingly sincere.) His wife's health fails as he recovers, and she finally succumbs in the course of their furious travels in search of experience. What perplexes the reader in all this, however, is that the narrator is constantly fascinated by adolescent boys without, for that, seeming to fulfill or repress this penchant. It can be argued that the narrator is conscious of his tastes but chooses to avoid more than a coy indication of them; others have maintained that his homosexuality is latent. In any case, the rather lyrical style of the novel, overly literary and poetic perhaps for the conveying of exact realities, does not incline one to either interpretation as against the other. This ambiguity seems, in the end, more baffling than rich in suggestion. The narrator of *La Symphonie pastorale* (1919), on the other hand, deceives only himself; Gide has seen to it that the reader has some frame of reference by which to read the book. The title of the novel refers as much to the pastor as to Beethoven; it is cast in the form of a journal but is most important for the way prose style incriminates the deceptive narrator, who fancies himself to be virtue incarnate. There are all sorts of archaisms in the prose—which may be intended to suggest a provincial French-Protestant milieu—but there are also frequent occurrences of unusual language serving as a verbal smoke screen in which the pastor envelops himself so as not to see reality. For example, auxiliary verbs such as *pouvoir* and *devoir* seem often to be used to no particular end: "J'eus une sorte de ravissement devant l'expression angélique que Gertrude put prendre soudain." Relative pronouns and subordinating conjunctions are repeated in the seventeenth-century manner that was considered cacophonous after Flaubert: "Et elle demeurait obtusément convaincue que ma peine était vaine; de sorte que naturellement il lui paraissait malséant que je consacrasse à cette oeuvre un temps qu'elle prétendait toujours qui serait mieux employé différemment. Et chaque fois que je m'occupais de Gertrude elle trouvait à me représenter que je ne sais qui ou quoi attendait cependant après moi, et que je distrayais pour celle-ci un temps que j'eusse dû donner à d'autres." Sometimes the sentence seems interminable: "Et si, providentiellement, je m'étais trouvé libre de mon temps ce jour-là, moi qui suis si requis d'ordinaire, le reproche d'Amélie était d'autant plus injuste qu'elle savait bien que chacun de mes enfants avait soit un travail à faire, soit quelque occupation qui le retenait, et qu'elle-même, Amélie, n'a point de goût pour la musique, de sorte que, lorsqu'elle disposerait de tout son temps, jamais il ne lui viendrait à l'idée d'aller au concert, lors même que celui-ci se donnerait à notre porte." Elsewhere, abstractions and periphrases ("Je ne pensais pas soumettre ta constance à une pareille épreuve . . .") abound.

This complex style with its wordiness, repetitions, periphrases, abstractions, and archaic constructions renders beautifully the elaborately confused mind of the pastor. His perceptions are constantly out of focus and reveal less the outside world than they reflect the notions of a hopelessly muddled man, whose private readings of the Bible and interpretations of the actions of others all press toward disaster. The more intricate the language, the less the pastor sees his bad faith in thinking he is not in love with Gertrude, while preventing his son from seeing her. What Gide has done is most interesting if we compare *La Symphonie pastorale* with earlier novels in which we detect bad faith—or merely foolishness—in the narrator. We cannot be sure what the abbé Prévost thought about Des Grieux or wanted us to feel, but Gide has anchored his narrative quite firmly into a tradition of religious and moral conceptions. This reference to something preexisting and *outside* the novel allows us to see it *not* as a criticism of Protestant thought—the simplistic conclusion—but as a drama of self-deception in which personal interpretations of the Bible lead to whatever a self-centered mind wants of them.

Gide wrote two important third-person narratives, which, while often considered less perfect than *La Symphonie pastorale*, are far more curious in their ambitions. *Les Caves du Vatican* (1914), like two other early pieces of fiction, was called a *sotie*, not a novel or *récit*, the latter term being saved for introspective works like *La Symphonie pastorale*. A *sotie* was a kind of medieval fools' festival, and Gide uses the term to designate a narrative in which the figures behave in a grotesque, caricatural fashion, at once too monomaniac and too sketchy for the realist tradition. *Les Caves* has a marvelously involved plot turning around the putative imprisonment of Pope Leo XIII by Freemasons and a swindlers' scheme to raise money to free him. The characters are mostly related but in some cases by marriage or illegitimate union so that both a certain tightness and element of coincidence obtain in the story. Narration is handled with considerable nonchalance: soliloquy, interior monologue, authorial comment on plot, and free indirect discourse mingle. At the same time, however, *Les Caves* has a most interesting element of larger design, which was to be, if not imitated, at least duplicated in various novels. Four of the five parts focus on one character so that the forward movement of the plot is coordinated with a shifting emphasis on characters. We have seen something of this in Zola, but here it becomes a more striking structural principle.

The last character to occupy the foreground in *Les Caves*, Lafcadio, does not fit into the same pattern of stylization as the others, and in this problem we shall find the greatest peculiarity in Gide's fiction, both here and in *Les Faux-Monnayeurs*. Lafcadio is not a funny bourgeois worshipping either His Holiness or the Lodge; he believes, perhaps from Nietzsche, in his absolute ability to exercise a godlike control over his destiny, even though the manifestations of this belief are sometimes absurd. Thorny, problematic reflections on free will and gratuitous acts occupy him, and they may, despite the

fact that many commentators treat them with utter seriousness, be designed merely to betoken an adolescent
passion for the old clichés of metaphysics. His murder of
Amédée—brother-in-law of his legitimate half brother,
a relation he is unaware of—suddenly removes him from
the field of comic characters, both for the reader and
narrator. A number of subsequent passages bring to mind
Raskolnikov's horrible memories and fantasies. It would
seem that Gide meant this new psychological convention seriously, but it contrasts strangely with the bulk of
the novel. Finally comes the oddest of all: the last two
pages echo the conclusion of the epilogue to *Crime and
Punishment:* "This could be the subject of a new story"
(Dostoievsky); "Here a new book begins" (Gide). The
hitherto obscure figure of Geneviève is brought forward
to play the role Sonya does in *Crime and Punishment.*
Gide obviously knew what odd juggling he was doing
with his characters' behavior and his attitude toward it;
our question is whether this was a freaky attempt at
novelty or corresponded to a sound esthetic. The case of
Les Faux-Monnayeurs will illustrate the problem more
amply.

Les Faux-Monnayeurs (1926) is a curious piece of
fictional technique in several respects: different conventions of point of view are juxtaposed; the plot, which
is rather complex, turns about in the course of the
book rather interestingly; and finally, the conception
and presentation of the characters vary enormously.
By Flaubert's criterion of continuity and smoothness in
narration, the novel is a monster. It remains to be seen,
however, if Gide did not very carefully calculate certain
of its odder aspects.

The opening chapters are told by an urbane voice
which owes a good deal to Stendhal but yet manages to

make very different sorts of remarks, while generally remaining in the sympathetic-ironic vein. His denials of omniscience are especially characteristic; a careful effort is being made to suggest improvisation. Thematically the work does not settle down very fast: Bernard and Olivier's resentment of their families does not yet have any clear direction. In the meantime a complicated series of coincidences affecting a circle of relatives and acquaintances provides elements of plot, if nothing else. Characters are delineated variously: while the adolescents are a bit vague in their aspirations, puppetlike, almost emblematic caricatures surround Vincent; the parents are more familiar stereotypic figures. The intrusional narrative voice keeps the book moving, but it is evident that a stronger figure is going to have to take the action in hand: Edouard will be, if not the novel's main character, the one who will hold it together.

Edouard's introduction into the narrative brings up further questions of technique and character portrayal. Along with letters, considerable use is made of Edouard's diary, as if Gide felt the difficulty of sustaining the third-person narration with interventions and fell back onto the familiar first-person devices he had used in earlier works. The diary, of course, makes us see a character quite differently from a third-person account, since the sympathetic-ironic commentator must yield to a voice who is himself a participant in the action. Furthermore the diarist relates and interprets other characters' acts: in this last respect we must observe that Edouard is, in keeping with his literary profession, an exceptionally skilled if traditional novelist. The serious presentation of a number of minor characters—Georges Molinier, the Vedels, or La Pérouse—which we find in the diary is in many ways superior in impact and the illusion of depth than what the narrating voice of the opening chapters achieves. It is difficult to imagine that urbane commentator understanding the dreary French-Protestant household of the Vedels, or the hopelessly neurotic little Boris. Edouard's sketches are incisive and penetrating, and introduce a new tone into the novel.

On the other hand, Edouard as participant differs considerably from Edouard the narrator or reflector. Unlike the typical diary writer in the French novel, he has little gift for introspection, not even self-deceptive introspection. His acuteness as an observer is regularly counterbalanced by a certain obtuseness or even stupidity when he formulates general ideas or thinks about the nature of his projected novel (which is *his Faux-Monnayeurs* not the one we are reading; Gide likes to throw off imperceptive readers, whom he further tempted with his own *Journal des Faux-Monnayeurs*, a somewhat disappointing record of stages in the novel's composition). Often Edouard's self-depiction seems to lack center or focus; his personal traits, such as his clumsy approach to the idea of fiction or his pederasty, emerge in fitful fashion; much of the time he is so bland, in good humor or bad, that he lacks all salience. Being a character without much personality who narrates himself, he is immune to the sharpening irony other characters are subjected to.

We have been considering primarily the ways of presenting characters in *Les Faux-Monnayeurs*. To conclude, it would be best to discuss the plot pattern from which these characters cannot be separated. At the beginning Bernard and Olivier are both setting out on courses which will estrange them from their families and fulfill the strong but vague adolescent urge to be themselves; the contrasts between them are brought out, and we assume them to be the main characters. A subplot involves the devil's temptation of Vincent, who is quick to yield. What actually happens to Bernard and Olivier does not, however, add up to much: the one finds himself attached to Edouard as a not very overworked secretary, the other becomes Passavent's boyfriend with some vague editorial duties. The rest of Part I is essentially concerned with Edouard's visits and recollections, which introduce various lesser characters. In the center of the novel Edouard dominates with his reflections and discussions, while Bernard if anything becomes somewhat lackluster. This talkative section, with its digressions on the novel and on psychoanalysis, makes the reader wonder exactly what the point was in beginning the novel with Bernard and Olivier, who seem increasingly unlikely to be able to carry the weight of the rest of it, which already shows signs of disintegrating. To a certain extent, their function, in Part III, appears to be reduced to circulating among other characters in order to provoke dialogue. Their stories are brought neatly enough to an end, but by this point the reader's interest and attention is being steadily attracted away from Olivier's homosexual preferences and Bernard's uneventful search for his identity by a group of characters who at first appeared completely incidental. The counterfeit coin discovered in Part II leads to an elaborate plot involving the Molinier family and the Vedel pension. It becomes clear in retrospect that the opening chapters have dealt with a kind of metaphorical counterfeiting of the personality while the ugly events at the end are a demonstration of the concrete results of literal counterfeiting added to figurative kinds (including, as Gide wanted us to see, the psychiatrist's counterfeit cure of

Boris). Even a detail like Vincent's being overcome by the devil who earlier tempted him constitutes a movement from the figurative to the concrete.

Despite the care with which Gide attempted to relate the first and third parts of *Les Faux-Monnayeurs*, it is evident that the difference in tone and narrative method (the intervening narrator intrudes very little in the later part of the book) makes them difficult to reconcile, but Gide clearly wanted to make the seemingly impossible transition from a light-hearted, stylized beginning to a highly somber and realistic ending: the union of Stendhal and Dostoievsky. Edouard's diary is the device he found to accomplish this, for in it various tones and kinds of material can mingle without appearing too heteroclite. Edouard is not the central character—there is none—for his somewhat fuzzy, indeterminate personality would obviate such a possibility, but his diary is the transitional device which holds the novel together. It is quite possible that Gide devised all the false clues about a novel called *Les Faux-Monnayeurs* in an attempt to give Edouard's mental life some consistency and conceal the extent to which the diary conveys a realistic reflection of the various characters. As a writer Edouard succeeds in bringing to life everyone except himself.

Gide's fiction tends to fail where Mauriac's succeeds: as we have seen, certain major characters in *Les Faux-Monnayeurs* are curiously out of focus. Edouard's pederasty is coyly hinted at but never explained in psychological detail; Bernard and Olivier, furthermore, have little reality in their sexual choices; Laura, finally, is one of the most poorly realized women in fiction. Mauriac's adolescents, on the other hand, suffer vividly with their pimples, their conflicts with their parents, and the anguish of awakening sensuality. Their reality is hideously concrete and objective, unlike that of Bernard and Olivier who are obviously Gide's fantasy creatures. Furthermore, Mauriac's women, young as well as middle-aged, are frequently among his most successfully drawn characters.

Mauriac's finest novels are only a handful among a rather large and quite uneven production; it is not that Mauriac ever wrote trash; he simply did not usually succeed in bringing together, in even amounts, the requisite needs of character portrayal, narrative technique, local color, moral truth, and stylistic finish. In each of his less perfect novels one can usually detect some imbalance among these various factors. This is especially true of Parisian scenes or characters: in their spurious glamour we are reminded of the "cosmopolitan" novels of Bourget or Larbaud. Those set in the Bordelais are more authentic.

Mauriac's two best novels—and the earliest among his well-known ones—are *Le Baiser au lépreux* and *Génitrix*, which are related not only in plot and characters, but also in their use of literary allusion. The thematics of *Le Baiser au lépreux* (1922) center around two texts (supported by numerous other references); they are Corneille's *Polyeucte* and Aphorism 260 of Nietzsche's *Beyond Good and Evil*, in which the theory of the two moralities is exposed: "In a tour through the many finer and coarser moralities which have hitherto prevailed or still prevail on the earth, I found certain traits recurring regularly together, and connected with one another, until finally two primary types revealed themselves to me, and a radical distinction was brought to light. There is a *master-morality* and *slave-morality*." When Jean Péloueyre reads these words near the beginning of the

novel, he immediately knows himself to be a slave and
resigns himself to it, until the moment a wife is proposed to him; he thereupon feels that a wife will make
him a master. Quite the opposite occurs, and in marriage
he suffers even more than before from his ugliness and
unworthiness. His stay in Paris is the result, and there he
discovers, as he watches the crowds on the street, that
no one looks like a master; they are all slaves. Finally the
Nietzschean motif is curiously transformed into Christian terms as Jean lies dying: "What a difference there
was between the shooter of magpies and this dying man
who was giving his life for the salvation of several other
persons. The curé sank down before Him whose secret
is to make slaves like unto God." In this quotation there
is a curious reference to Jean's indirectly saving others,
and this brings us to the Polyeucte theme. *Polyeucte* is a
play that often disconcerts present-day readers because,
as Polyeucte is martyred, the other main characters, even
the foolish, meanspirited old Félix, suddenly are touched
by grace and become Christians. This would not have
seemed unmotivated to a pious seventeenth-century
spectator, because he would have realized that what is
occurring is the so-called "reversiblity" of grace: the
saints enjoy so great a quantity of grace that it can
pour down even upon sinners, and, in the case of Polyeucte, it is perfectly seemly that his wife, father-in-law,
and even his supposed enemy, Sévère, should be converted by his grace. Thus Mauriac's use of allusions to
the play, which include transforming the line "Mon
Polyeucte touche à son heure dernière" to "Mon Péloueyre touche à son heure dernière." Jean, the leper of the
title, by caring for his dying friend, has acquired so
much grace as to sustain those in his milieu after his
death.

In discussing the texture of *Le Baiser au lépreux*, we might best begin with its imagery. Descriptions are very numerous, even for Mauriac, whose insistence on atmosphere is one of his dominant traits. Seasons, storms, heat, cold, odors, landscape, and the characteristics of each hour of the day in the Landes with its resinous pine forests recur with endless variations. Mostly these have no more portentous symbolic value than the traditional relation between the *I* and the landscape of romantic poetry. For example, disquiet characters hear the Atlantic roar in the distance during equinoctial storms, or, elsewhere, M. Jérôme's yearning for eternal rest is connected with the ocean of death. Sometimes, however, an image becomes a judgment, an authorial intrusion as when, at the end of the wedding night, Noémi seems a sleeping martyr, and "One should have kissed her feet, seized this tender body, and, without waking her, holding her just as she was, run toward the deep sea, give her over to the chaste foam." Mauriac's images thus tend often to slip back and forth between description and commentary. After Jean, in a passage in free indirect discourse, thinks of himself as a sow bug (*cloporte*, a common term of denigration in French), we find a scene, switching characteristically to a dramatic present, which begins: "There is no one left in the darkened room, as if some entomological experiment were about to take place, save this little black male, timid before the marvelous female. . . . The virgin observes this larva who is her destiny." Later the insect image occurs to Noémi as she hears crickets chirping.

Aside from the curious shifts from description to symbol, metaphor, or commentary, the texture of the novel is further complicated by a highly ambiguous blending of ordinary narrative, free indirect discourse, and a kind of sympathetic, involved judgment on the characters. This latter characteristic is perhaps what separates Mauriac most from similar ambiguities in Flaubert, although it must also be pointed out that subtle transitions within a paragraph are more peculiar to Mauriac. Here are some examples: "[Jean has gone into the garden in the late afternoon.] Cadette's grandson was watering the lettuce—a handsome brute, feet bare in his clogs, beloved of all the girls and shunned by Jean Péloueyre, who was ashamed to be the Master: should not *he* have been the sickly servant of this young and triumphant garden god? Even at a distance he dared not smile at him; with peasants his shyness turned to paralysis." Mauriac's style, with its elegant, but not grandiloquent rhythms and its great precision and evocativeness of vocabulary, amalgamates what Jean first sees, what he feels but could not express so well—no colloquialisms identify this as true free indirect discourse—and the heightened poetic reference ("triomphant et juvénile dieu potager"), which is so characteristic of Mauriac. The question is an especially interesting device since it belongs at once to free indirect discourse and to the interventional style.

Our next example shows the tenuous line of demarcation in Mauriac between free indirect discourse and something approaching *monologue intérieur:* "The strange thing was that he no longer felt anything of his feelings from the days when at High Mass Noémi rustled up the aisle in her crisp dress. He kept shaking his head so as not to think of that September night when she would be given over to him. That night will never come: war will break out, someone will die, there will be an earthquake." Mauriac's narrative shifts to the first person are always quite dramatically planned, but here the effect is intensified by the unexpected future tense of what has become a first-person inner exclamation.

In the long paragraph following our last quote, there is an interesting, if understated, alternation of voices. First Noémi wonders "what the cricket would do with her," and then her mother arrives to console her:

> Then she assured her that in these matters you had to rely on your priest; now, hadn't the curé himself chosen marriage for her? A housewifely little soul, all tenderness and piety, Noémi might have not replied anything. She didn't read novels, she assumed her share of the house-keeping, she obeyed. She was told that men have no need of being handsome, that marriage produces love like a peachtree peaches. But it would have been enough, in order to convince her, to repeat the axiom: "You don't turn down a Péloueyre."

In an economical few lines, by lapsing into what we might call *impersonal* free indirect discourse, her whole *fiançailles* are subsumed. We do not know who, in particular, offers her this or that piece of advice, once her mother's voice is unambiguously finished; the last sentence sounds like a kind of public social judgment, since it is hypothetical in form, if vehement in import. Or it may perfectly well be the author's ironic comment on the milieu Noémi lives in. The fusion of mother, public, and author is so complete as to leave one undecided.

Génitrix (1923) is a companion novel to *Le Baiser au lépreux* in that it treats of the other half of the Péloueyre family, Félicité Cazenave, née Péloueyre, and her son Fernand. This side of the clan is anticlerical, ends as literally sterile as the other, but enjoys no benefit of grace. The description, in *Le Baiser au lépreux*, of Félicité as an "old Juno" suggests the classical direction literary allusion will take in this work: the word *Génitrix* (used only once in the text), suggests the great mother of the Roman people, Venus, and Fernand calls Félicité, with unconscious irony, "le type achevé d'une fondatrice de race." Later, after her death, she appears to Fernand in a most Virgilian fashion, and, at this point, he is described as an "aging Aeneus." She is elsewhere a "she-wolf," the nurse of Romulus and Remus, and therefore a secondary mother to Rome.

Many other supporting references to antiquity occur: Fernand is an idol, a Terminus god, and, finally, as his mother—the goddess, Maenad, Medusa, and murdered Agrippina—takes hold of him, he becomes the hoary Juno his mother had been earlier. They are both, furthermore, descendants of the pagan, sun-worshipping, *landais* shepherds of the early nineteenth century. The first three chapters, dealing with Mathilde's death, each end on the vision of a bank or shore, which a river or sea—the Acheron—separates from the realm of the dead. And when ladies come to call afterward, they expect something to eat which might calm the Shades. Set against these pagan survivals, we find Félicité's agony at the Evangelical third hour, and the old servant Marie de Lados, the "black virgin," replacing her in the end as Maria Genitrix—and consolatrix.

Certain tendencies in narrative technique differentiate *Génitrix* from *Le Baiser au lépreux*. The use of present-tense interior monologue in the second person is especially interesting: "It's too late to deceive yourself. No shivering yet, but so great a sensation of coldness that you try, without much success, to believe it comes from the night wind and the chilly sweat on your limbs. You chose your own bad luck. . . ." This form of interior monologue is best suited for recollections and moral meditations as opposed to the first-person one Dujardin used to record the impact of the exterior world. It also allows a certain ambiguity when it is used, as Mauriac does, in conjunction with the narrator's addressing his characters (the device Charles-Louis Phillippe especially liked); here Fernand's past-tense free indirect discourse is interrupted by the author: "His wonderful mother! Why had a sneering little schoolteacher had the nerve to stand in his way? Mathilde, whose ghost was also seated at this table, far from the fire, in a draft, as when you were alive, death no longer deifies you." This is an odd sequence of persons, quite solecistic by any normal criterion, but immensely effective in the way it heightens the feeling of Mathilde's moral presence. Elsewhere Mauriac creates prestidigious shifts in center of consciousness among his characters:

> Thus absorbed, she [Félicité] was startled by Fernand's footsteps in the vestibule and heard him ask Marie de Lados if lunch was served. Since fifteen minutes remained before lunch, he went into the garden. Félicité, behind the curtains, spied on him. He was standing in the middle of the path. What was he looking at? His mother hardly imagined that he saw, in his mind, the room in the rue Huguerie where, once a month, his regular girl had expected him. Terrycloth towels were always drying on a line at the window. She called him her old tightwad because you couldn't get a penny out of him beyond the agreed-on price.

The sentence "what was he looking at" is the pivotal one in this passage. As we have seen before, questions often perform a modulatory role in moving about from point of view to point of view, since they suggest, in the answer, material that has previously been out of reach of the reader. Curiously enough, the other device most characteristic of oratory, the exclamation, is also part and parcel of Mauriac's shifting narration. Here is an extraordinarily elliptic example of its function: "All the wives, both on the Péloueyre and on the Cazenave side, were the kind who whisper to their husbands: 'Get it over with.' Inevitably, however, there appears one day

on one link of the family chain a spot of rust which
begins to gnaw away. Unfortunate are they who come
after. O poor hearts as yet unborn! My children, what
have I bequeathed you!" The exclamations are not, obviously, the narrator's, nor can they be Félicité's: it is a
hypothetical voice which speaks, a voice hovering between the author and characters, representing neither,
but a moral party to the action.

Two other Mauriac novels deserve mention for their
techniques. *Le Noeud de vipères* (1932) has the stylistic
distinction of the earlier novels, but it reveals Mauriac's
inability to weave a true fictional illusion within the con-
fines of the diary-novel. The strictly limited point of
view which the genre demands runs quite counter to
Mauriac's basic tendency to slip in and out of his characters' minds. The relative failure of *Le Noeud de
vipères* thus provides a sort of negative proof of the
dominant traits of Mauriac's imagination.

In *Thérèse Desqueyroux* (1927) we find again the
imagery characteristic of Mauriac's *landais* novels; if
anything, even more intense use is made of fire, water,
heat, cold, season, and silence. The last is especially important since it is not only part of the landscape but also
part of the plot: the characters are engaged in *faire le
silence*, in hushing up scandal. The most unusual thing
about *Thérèse*, however, is its narrative structure. The
first two-thirds of the novel consist of a short journey by
carriage and train during which Thérèse travels back
into the past searching for some pattern in her life, for
some reason why she should have tried to poison her
husband. The narrative is formed of short sections, not
necessarily in strict chronological order and ranging in
technique from present-tense interior monologue to past-
tense free indirect discourse and external narration; the

persons alternate between first and third. Mauriac's characteristic fondness for building his novels out of small
subsections, each with its own striking effect of description, metaphor, or dialogue, is reinforced here by the
unifying device of the train trip which, obtruding here
and there, gives a feeling of progression and goal to the
episode, while still permitting most of the plot to unfold
haphazardly in Thérèse's point of view, although not
with absolute consistency: his aim is to create a general
impression, as Balzac often did, rather than to make of
a method a straitjacket. However, this brings up an important problem: the rest of the book depends on a de-
cision—to release Thérèse—which only Bernard can
make and which somehow must be motivated by something more than the fear that Anne's marriage will be
endangered. Mauriac elegantly solves this dilemma. Instead of our being placed in the center of Bernard's cogi-
tations, we are simply presented with one allusive image
that flashes into his mind as he first sees Thérèse after the
winter of her incarceration: "Bernard was to remember,
many years later, that, as this broken body approached,
he first thought: Criminal Court. But that was not because of Thérèse's crime. In a split second he saw again
the colored illustration in the *Petit Parisien*, which,
among many others, decorated the wooden outhouse in
the garden at Argelouse—and, while flies buzzed and
outside the cicadas chirped in the flaming light, he, a
child still, examined the red and green picture which
showed the Prisoner of Poitiers." With the passage of
time, this allusion has become dimmer: it refers to a
famous trial in 1901 brought by the police against a
woman and her son who had kept her daughter a prisoner (*séquestrée*) for some twenty-five years after the
daughter had given birth to an illegitimate baby (Gide

wrote about the case in *Ne jugez pas*). The facts of the
situation are obviously different, but Bernard senses that
he has been a party, much abetted by the sinister old
servants, to the crime of sequestration. Everything Bernard feels is implied in the most economical fashion; we
need no further explanation.

With the last chapter of *Thérèse*, where she and
Bernard part in Paris, the themes of the opening chapters
return: there is a distinct cyclical movement in the novel
as she finally has the conversation with him that she had
expected to have on returning to Argelouse in the early
chapters. But this explanation of motives takes an ironic
form: Bernard can neither believe that she poisoned
him for his property nor that some obscure and chance
impulse led her to it. The novel ends with an unanswer-
able question, one which Mauriac, in the brief meditation which prefaces the novel, had put forth by quoting
Baudelaire's great prose-poem "Mademoiselle Bistouri":
"Lord, have pity on madmen; O Creator! can there
exist monsters in the eyes of Him who knows why they
exist, how they came about, and how they could not
have been?"

The use of deceptive first-person narrative and authorial intervention in the early decades of this century
produced a number of novels that are as strikingly varied
in their specific handling of these techniques as they are
in their styles, for each of the writers we have been
examining was a master of French prose. They, furthermore, have little in common with regard to thematic
material; while religious preoccupations were shared by
Philippe, Mauriac, and Gide, the latter's lengthy pieces
of fiction do not reflect them, and Alain-Fournier's
childhood piety was transformed into a secular, para-
Christian mystique of the kind found in the symbolists.

That they all began their careers as poets toward the end of a great age in French poetry is perhaps their most significant bond. For each of them had first conceived of the highest literature as something far more intense than any mere story could be; they had considered lyricism to be the essence of literary art, a quality that, while it might be present in prose—as the invention of the prose-poem had shown—risked being hopelessly diluted in the prevailing conventions of the novel. Valéry's famous dismissal of fiction as containing intolerable sentences like "The Marquise went out at 5 o'clock" represents one not uncharacteristic symbolist attitude, just as Des Esseintes had felt the novel was to be replaced by the prose-poem, which would be a kind of concentrated essence of fiction. It is exactly this kind of poet's thinking, therefore, that we can consider the determining factor in the various kinds of fictional forms devised by the major postnaturalist novelists. There had existed, to be sure, a few works sometimes called "symbolist novels," of which Gide's *Le Voyage d'Urien* is one, but they had failed signally to capture any of the intensity of poetry, just as they had failed to renew narrative technique. On the other hand, the novelist of the postnaturalist period whose theories of art and style (art as religion, style as metaphor) most resemble those of the symbolists escapes our generalization since he had been little tempted by verse: Marcel Proust was incomparably the greatest novelist of the period and, starting from the basis of first-person narrative, invented so complex a novel form that it must be examined by itself.

6

Proust and First-Person Narration

PROUST'S NOVEL IS EXCEPTIONAL with respect to the previous traditions of French fiction in at least two ways. First of all, it presents a vast picture of society, much as Balzac and Zola did, but within the context of a first-person novel. Until Proust's time it had been assumed, perhaps unconsciously, that first-person narration was suitable only for relatively short works and intimate subjects. The traditional *I* of narration could hardly have gotten out of himself sufficiently to undertake a description of social structure in vast detail. In the second place, the *I* of *A la recherche du temps perdu* resembles in no way that of the confession novel, with his highly selective, rather orderly memories or the deceptive narrator, whose author must manipulate him with subtle strategy in order to inform the reader covertly about his wrongheadedness. The awareness of Proust's narrator encompasses not only society, in the large as well as the narrow sense, but extends to such fringes of perception that the narrative method has been at times compared to stream-of-consciousness technique. The comparison is faulty, however, since, rather than existing in one plane of time or knowledge, Proust's narrator is erratic, in turn omniscient, deceptive, deceived, or ignorant. And despite our quickly becoming familiar with his nervous tics and constant health worries, with his recurrent patterns of disappointment and disaffection, he eludes us just as he eludes himself: the novel consists of a quest for truth and stability, which will only be reached in the closing pages where the narrator paradoxically sets out to write the novel we have read. A la recherche has, furthermore, an elaborate intellectual armature which justifies the peculiar presentation of the narrator and his life.

The opening of Du Côté de chez Swann breaks completely with earlier conventions of first-person fiction. The first sentence, "For a long time I went to bed early" (the tense in French is especially peculiar [1]), does not situate us in any discernible time; as a matter of fact we are embarking on a prodigious looping back which will only be closed (though never explicitly so) and gone beyond in the middle of the last part of A la recherche. But the narrator is in no haste to begin his story: all periods in his life are jumbled together as he lies awake, and the prose moves forward in a highly associative manner. Dreams and the state of half-wakefulness are, as we shall see, parts of a series of special and precious experiences in which time and ordinary reality recede from our consciousness.

With no real transition or explanation of why he is beginning there, the narrator tells of his childhood anguish at going to bed, and gradually begins to focus on a particular evening (the movement back and forth from iterative-imperfect time to punctual time is very char-

[1] See Roger Shattuck, *Proust's Binoculars, A Study of Memory, Time, and Recognition in "A la recherche du temps perdu"* (New York, 1963), 79–83.

acteristic of Proust) when Swann came to dine at Combray. The literal account of this episode—the narrator is
sent to bed by his father without his mother's kiss, attempts to send a note to her during the dinner, and goes
to wait for her on the stair landing at the end of the
evening—is accompanied by an extraordinary metaphorical embellishment, which is quite morbid and strangely
para-Freudian. The narrator fancies his mother in the
midst of an "inconceivable, infernal rejoicing," sur-
rounded by "alluring, perverted, hostile throngs," who
are "initiating" her into "cruel mysteries" and "unheard
of raptures." The theme of erotic jealousy continues:
when the mother climbs the stairs and sees the narrator,
she gasps, "Run, so your father won't see you . . . ,"
and, as the latter arrives, becomes "embarrassed" and
"timid" like someone who had done something very
wrong, like a penitent adulteress caught in the act. The
night the narrator subsequently spends with his mother,
at his father's casual behest, seems to him "a victory
against her," and he imagines her aging and dying. The
figurative breaking of the taboo against incest, and the
fit punishment of one of the partners by death, is, of
course, congruent with psychoanalytic conceptions of
childhood emotive life, despite the fact that Proust knew
nothing of this aspect of Freud's thought.

The "bedtime drama," which remains in the narrator's
conscious memories, leads him, by contrast, to the resur-
rection of the rest of his childhood at Combray through
the taste of the madeleine cookie soaked in linden tea and
consequent involuntary memory. This famous passage
has, as Proust pointed out, antecedents in Chateaubriand,
Nerval, and Baudelaire; the importance of involuntary
memory is that, like awakening or the experience of mu-
sic, it jars us loose from factual existence. The episode

takes place "one day," somewhere in later time—but before the end of the novel—and constitutes the *single* demonstration in the novel of the principle amply set forth at the end that broad areas of the past will rise into mind through involuntary memory.

The Combray which arises out of the cup of linden tea is dense in its offerings to the senses, and the sentences which describe it are often among the most characteristic ones in Proust. Repeated modifiers, relative clauses, adjectives, or appositions are frequent; here are, for example, "smells natural enough indeed . . . but already humanized, domesticated, confined, an exquisite, skillful, limpid jelly, blending all the fruits of the year which have left the orchard for the storeroom, seasonal ones but plenishing and home-loving, compensating for the sharpness of hoar frost with the sweet savor of warm bread, lazy ones and punctual as a village clock, roving ones and pious." Elsewhere the associative movement of Proust's prose is exemplified by a long sentence with many subordinate clauses which keep adding incisive detail but have little logical justification:

> . . . when on Sundays I saw [the steeple] . . . blaze . . . I would know exactly the color of the sunlight upon the Square, the heat and dust of the market, the shadow made by the blinds of the shop into which Mama would perhaps go on her way to mass, penetrating its odor of unbleached cotton, to purchase a handkerchief or something, of which the draper himself would let her see what he had, bowing from the waist: who, having made everything ready for shutting up, had just gone into the back shop to put on his Sunday coat and to wash his hands, which it was his habit . . . to rub one against the other with an air of enterprise, cunning, and success.

Normally subordination indicates just that: something which is logically dependent on something else; but here the draper's tics are more fully realized than the sunlight on the square. Proust's tentacular syntax draws things together into imaginative wholes with little regard for rational connection; in that respect its order resembles much poetry of the same period.

The shifting, unstable quality of associational movement in sentences is paralleled in the second chapter of "Combray" by an odd temporal pattern, one perhaps unmatched in fiction: it can most easily be described as a conflation, the simultaneous presentation of three units of time: day, season, and year.

A large part of "Combray" takes place on a Sunday. There are references to arriving "the last week before Easter," to saying good morning to Aunt Léonie before mass, to mass, to meeting Legrandin, who comes to Combray only "from Saturday evening to Monday morning," and, finally, a direct mention of Sunday. Sunday's events include mass, lunch, reading in the garden, a parade of soldiers, a storm, and the curé's visit to Aunt Léonie. There is a unifying theme and one unifying character in this disparate assortment of episodes: Aunt Léonie is the first and last character we see, and throughout the day she is obsessed with curiosity as to whether or not Mme Goupil arrived at mass after the elevation. She speculates about this with Françoise, interrogates her relatives back from church, and awaits with anxiety the late-afternoon visit of Eulalie, who is certain to be informed of such matters. Eulalie's visit, however, coincides with that of the curé, and in the confusion of having so many callers, Aunt Léonie forgets to enquire about Mme Goupil.

This Sunday would not, on the surface, seem to be a very unusual piece of narrative, were it not for one fact: it is written, with the exception of an occasional anecdote, in the imperfect tense. Even the verbs of saying, specific though the conversation be, are in the imperfect:

> "Françoise, just imagine, Mme Goupil went by over fifteen minutes late to get her sister; if she loses any more time on the way I shouldn't be surprised if she gets there after the elevation."
>
> "Well, there would be nothing odd about that," would be the answer.
>
> "Françoise, if you had come in five minutes ago, you would have seen Mme Imbert go by with a bunch of asparagus twice the size of what the Callot woman sells. . . ."
>
> "I shouldn't be surprised if they came from the curé's," Françoise would say.
>
> "Oh, really, Françoise," my aunt would reply.

Proust's continual presentation of the particular as the general throughout this Sunday is a charming device; each *would say, would reply, would sigh* introducing a quotation delights the ear by its insistence on the endlessly iterative cycle of life in Combray and its apotheosis of the trivial.

This use of the imperfect has even further implications, for by the vagueness of this tense Proust is not simply suggesting the melting together of all Combray Sundays, but also the merging of larger patterns of time. The first temporal unit we notice in Combray is the day; there is superimposed upon it, however, the progress of the season. The narrator arrives at Eastertime when the weather is still cold. Shortly afterwards Françoise and Aunt Léonie talk of asparagus, which Françoise has been serving a great deal of late. Asparagus becomes plentiful in France only in late April and May, when the weather is already warm. Somewhat later the weather is too hot. As the storm comes on, Aunt Léonie is amazed that there is so little light at four-thirty in the afternoon, "a week before Rogation Days." Since Rogation Days immediately precede Ascension Day, which is forty days after Easter, we are far in time from the beginning of this morning. The day and the season pursue their course in parallel fashion: nine o'clock is in March, five o'clock in May. The multiple facets of life in Combray, as it varies with the hour and the month, could hardly be more imaginatively and economically rendered. After the Sunday time pattern has come to an end, the seasonal one continues. On Saturdays in May the narrator's family goes to the *mois de Marie*, and finally it is summer. Toward the end of "Combray" the pattern of narrative becomes more geographical than temporal. The "Côté de Méséglise" and the "Côté de Guermantes" become the organizing principles. Nevertheless, there is some question of leaving Combray and finally of an autumn which the narrator spends there.

In addition to the progress of the day and season in Combray there is a further dimension of time lapse: the years. The most apparent example of the passing years is found in the portrayal of Aunt Léonie. During Sunday and spring she remains exceptionally lively despite her self-claustration. Even the latter is not complete since she still moves from one of her two rooms to the other in order to permit tidying and airing. Premature old age weighs heavy on her, however, as the summer wears on, and she has withdrawn more and more: she can no longer go into her second room because of atony and she no longer receives any visitors at all. Finally, we learn that Aunt Léonie is dead, but in a typically Proustian use of tense: "But I got into the habit of walking alone on those days, in the Méséglise-la-Vineuse direction, in that autumn we'd been obliged to come to Combray to settle my Aunt Léonie's estate, for she had, after all these years, died." The aunt's actual death is not at first described; we are suddenly brought into a new time focus where her death is a past event, mentioned casually as a subordinate, explanatory matter. The precise passage of the years is never insisted on in "Combray" by numbering them, but the events of the season fall into a pattern parallel to those of the years. Léonie can poetically die only in autumn, for, as she is the member of the family most associated with Combray, she, like the village, must vanish from our minds with the return to Paris, the city of winter life.

Here and there in "Combray," and especially toward the end, the narrator is tormented by certain problems of philosophical import which he sets forth both as they occurred to him in childhood and as he analyzes them from a mature viewpoint. The child narrator feels constantly drawn toward forms of beauty—esthetic pleasure in nature, descriptions in books, evocative names like the "orange" one of Guermantes—but he is also frustrated when he cannot tell why a landscape enchants him or when he sees that the Duchesse de Guermantes is merely a woman devoid of any orange aura. He is making the mistake of imagining that beauty lies in things rather than in our own subjective perceptions of them. As the adult narrator points out, true reality, which is subjective, can best be apprehended in imagination, involuntary memories of the past, dreams, or works of art, where no ordinary physical facts confuse us as to the source of beauty.

This form of subjective idealism derives from Kant—and, for its esthetic emphasis, from Schopenhauer as well; the distinction between phenomena and noumena is the essential one. A particular aspect of Kant's thought which underwent special elaboration in Proust was the

Thing-in-Itself. If, as Kant maintained, we perceive things through the familiar categories of time, causality, space, and so forth, we deform everything, and know nothing of the object we attempt to perceive. Proust adapts this unknowability of the Thing-in-Itself to the mystery of another person's subjectivity, which is totally inaccessible to us, and he creates narrative patterns in which we feel a certain malaise about what is going on in a character-in-himself. "Un Amour de Swann" is the first major demonstration of this principle.

This middle part of *Du Côté de chez Swann* is the only part of *A la recherche* written in the third person, and, as befits this peculiarity, has an unusual function in the novel's structure. The story of Swann's love for Odette, which feeds on jealousy, is a transposition into ordinary sexual terms of the bedtime drama, and a number of comparisons are made between the two. It is also a prefiguration, in one way or another, of all the love affairs in the novel, and most specifically of the narrator's liaison with Albertine. Taking place before the narrator's birth, it warns us of what to expect, and gradually, as the narrator learns more and more about Swann and Odette's past, comes to convince him of the inevitability of his own experience in love. Proust chooses, in this one case, to provide the reader with information the narrator will only acquire slowly, although he also characteristically disconcerts the reader by making a complete break between the story of Swann in love and that of Swann's later married life, which follows. This break completes the demonstration of the mystery of the Other, for, while we, following the point of view of Swann maintained in the third-person narrative section, realize, with him, that Odette is unknowable, we also learn that personality is discontinuous, unpredictable, and unstable.

There will be countless examples in *A la recherche* of characters exhibiting unsuspected traits or some usually considered mutually exclusive. In a sense there is no psychology in Proust nor any serious theoretical possibility of one.

The narrative which begins with the last part of *Swann* and continues through *A l'ombre* carries further the narrator's mistaken quest for beauty in things, places, and girls. Some interesting elements of narrative time can be observed here. Proust carefully organizes his episodes, almost throughout the novel, around the cycle of the seasons, but these may be elliptically presented. For example, the first part of *A l'ombre* covers two winters, with no mention of an intervening summer, since summer would involve vacations and separation from Gilberte. The second part, on the other hand, consists, by contrast, of a summer at the coast. In it we find an example of a complicated time pattern related to the one we examined in "Combray" but different from it in that weaving in and out between iterative-imperfect tense and punctual preterite, as well as between days and months, is more noticeable. Furthermore, this passage is shaped as a kind of *looping forward* in time, the reverse of the looping back we have found in Balzac and Zola.

The episode of dinner at Rivebelle begins on a particular day when the narrator is alone because Saint-Loup is on duty at Doncières; they plan, however, to meet for dinner. He sees the band of *jeunes filles en fleurs* for the first time, and then goes to his room to nap before dressing for dinner. The season is midsummer, and so far the narrative chronology is conventional. Then, as he enters his room, the narrator describes the quality of light in the sky and on the sea, only to pursue with visions of a later month: "Soon the days grew shorter

. . . ." Passage of time is further indicated: "A few
weeks later when I would get back to my room it was
dark . . . ." Notice that Proust is not saying "it *would
be* dark . . ."; the reader automatically assumes that,
in typical fashion, the narrator is skipping over intervening episodes. Suddenly, however, we are brought
back to punctual linear time: "there was a knock at the
door," and a member of the hotel staff enters to answer
a question that was asked a few weeks and a few pages
earlier. Imperfect tenses yield abruptly to perfect, and
situate us back into midsummer. Then, "early in the
season when we would arrive at Rivebelle" introduces
the dinner episode, and it also moves forward in time,
through imperfects, from the days when they arrive
at the restaurant before nightfall, to the period when
it is already dark. In the same ambiguous tense the narrator dines, returns to the hotel, falls asleep, and awak-
ens. But as he wakes up, he remembers something in a
perfect tense, the *passé simple*, which implies a definite
day; a page later we learn that "that day" when he
awoke, was the one following the day he first saw the
jeunes filles en fleurs. In other words real chronology
is a point of departure for future situations, but in cyclical fashion we return to the starting point. To be sure,
this technique does not always demand such careful
reading of tenses; frequently Proust merely says, "But
to get back to . . . ." Whether subtle or not, this inclu-
sive presentation of episodes with little regard for chronology is essential to Proust's imagination.

Perhaps the greatest narrative function of the looping
forward and alternate iterative-preterite narration is to
effect an unobtrusive transition between quite different
thematic areas: the Mme de Villeparisis–Saint-Loup–
Charlus complex yields to the band of girls, without the

reader's feeling that one subject has simply been dropped for another. Another way of holding together seemingly disparate material is the long-day pattern we have seen in Balzac. Part I of *Le Côté de Guermantes*, a distinctly new narrative unit, beginning in autumn after the summer at Balbec and devoted primarily to the author's continued exploration of aristocratic society, concludes with an interminable morning and afternoon in the spring, during which, essentially, the narrator has lunch with Saint-Loup and Rachel, goes with them to the theater, and attends Mme de Villeparisis' party. Endless, seemingly incidental material is brought in. The same might be said of the Duchesse de Guermantes' dinner party (in the second part of *Le Côté de Guermantes*) which is followed by a late visit to Charlus. Both days are constructed around public and private appearances of members of the Guermantes family, but they do not seem to have any greater thematic organization. The same cannot, however, be said of a third subsequent long day, which follows somewhat precipitously on the dinner party (the dinner is in winter; two months later the narrator receives an invitation for a party that will not take place until about June: Proust is accelerating time). This third long day includes the visit to the duke and duchess at the end of *Le Côté de Guermantes* (during which the narrator sees the duke rebuff Swann), the postponed account of Charlus' behavior with Jupien that afternoon, the party at the Princesse de Guermantes', and ends with an after-midnight visit from Albertine. All the episodes are designed to show characters in a new and generally unfavorable light, especially the duke, duchess, and baron, while society in general is oddly illuminated by the "oriental," that is, crescent, sodomitic moon hanging over Paris that evening. Furthermore, the digressions entailed by the party scene exemplify the curious temporal density they often create in Proust. Each character has, bound to his present appearance, the dimensions of what he was, what he is to others, and what he will be. Thus, in the course of the Princesse de Guermantes' soirée, the narrator informs us of the background of most of the guests and anticipates the *déclassement* of the Baron de Charlus, the Princess' attachment to him, and the gradual decline of the Guermantes' social position. These digressions are not mere excrescenses; they deepen our sense of the present situation, which assumes the poignant character of a last great appearance of the Guermantes in society when they are still supreme in the Faubourg Saint-Germain. Much of the material presented in this fashion would otherwise, of course, be recalcitrant to exposition; we must think of the Princess' soirée as a magnetic field which holds together all this indispensable information.

In contrast to the long days and ample chapters we associate with Proust there are five short marked-off sections in *A la recherche* which form perhaps the essential moral-thematic articulations of the work. One is the first chapter of "Combray" with the bedtime drama and the madeleine episode which we have examined; another, the death of the grandmother, occurs near the middle of *Le Côté de Guermantes*, but its real significance can be seen only retrospectively. Three such sections occur in *Sodome et Gomorrhe*. Part I of *Sodome*, the introduction to men-women, reveals an even greater kind of depravity (for Proust regarded it as such) than the various forms of vice with which the aristocracy has been more and more associated since the grandmother's death. The thematic design is clear: while it is she who unwittingly, through her acquaintance with

Mme de Villeparisis, gave him an entrée into society, it is only after her tutelary influence is gone that the narrator will see the fashionable world with all its flaws. The innocent quest for beauty which informed *Swann* and *A l'ombre* has given way to the ugliness of experience. In the brief "intermittences du coeur" which closes Part II, Chapter 1 of *Sodome,* the narrator has a final recollection of his grandmother and her moral integrity before he finds himself involved in the cities of the plain through his attachment to Albertine. With the last short section, Part II, Chapter 4 of *Sodome,* many thematic strands are brought together—the bedtime drama, murder of a parent, Swann in love, and Mlle Vinteuil at Montjouvain are evoked in close order:

> At the sound of these words, uttered as we were entering the Parville station, so far from Combray and Montjouvain, so long after the death of Vinteuil, an image stirred in my heart, an image which I had kept in reserve for so many years that even if I had been able to guess, when I stored it up, long ago, that it had a noxious power, I should have thought that in the course of time it had entirely lost it; preserved alive in the depths of my being —like Orestes whose death the gods had prevented in order that, on the appointed day, he might return to his native land to punish the murderers of Agamemnon—as expiation, as a retribution (who can tell?) for my having allowed my grandmother to die, perhaps; rising up suddenly from the night in which it seemed forever buried, and striking, like an Avenger, in order to inaugurate for me a new, terrible, and justly deserved existence, perhaps also to make dazzlingly clear to my eyes the fatal consequences which evil actions indefinitely engender, not only for those who have committed them, but for those who have done no more, have thought that they were doing no more than look on at a curious and entertaining spectacle, like myself, alas, on that afternoon long ago at Montjouvain, concealed behind a bush where (as when

I was complacently to listen to an account of Swann's love affairs), I had perilously allowed to open within myself the fatal road, destined to cause me suffering, of Knowledge. . . . It was Trieste, it was that unknown world in which I could feel that Albertine took a delight, in which lay her memories, her friendships, her childish loves, that exhaled that hostile, inexplicable atmosphere, like the atmosphere that used to waft up to my bedroom in Combray from the dining room where I could hear, talking and laughing with strangers, amid the clatter of forks and knives, Mama who would not be coming upstairs to say good night to me; like the atmosphere that had filled for Swann the houses to which Odette went at night in search of inconceivable joys.

From now on the novel will bear primarily on the narrator; society has been explored and has contaminated him finally with its vices and dire wisdom.

There are two interesting examples of what one might call parallel-contrastive narratives in *Sodome* and *La Prisonnière;* one deals with taking the train to a dinner party at the Verdurins' rented house near Balbec, the other with a day at home in Paris. In *Sodome* the narrator and other guests take the train from Balbec, find Charlus at the Verdurins' for the first time, and return home, partly by coach. Somewhat later on, toward the end of the summer, they again board the train—but this time in the iterative-imperfect tense—find Charlus already installed, and, with constant shifts between specific anecdote and imperfect narration—Charlus' reading a Balzac novel is the motif that unites the two time planes —journey toward a dinner party that is not described. Their return home, this time by train, is amply detailed, however, and consists of a series of stories, each one attached to a station on the train line. The parallel-contrastive narration in *La Prisonnière*, on the other hand, is exclusively based on tense distinction. Most of this section of *A la recherche* takes place on two days, which the narrator largely spends at home, but with one little social outing on each (this pattern of a social occasion interrupting a period of introspection can already be seen in Swann's appearance at Mme de Sainte-Euverte's musicale; it is frequent in Proust). The two days are quite different, however, in that the first one is a generalized day, written in the imperfect tense, and the second, which, by some elaborate juggling of time notation, occurs two days later, takes place on a very specific Sunday in February and is the most protracted long-day narration in *A la recherche*. It is the one during which we follow, hour by hour, the narrator's obsessive jealous concern over Albertine's activities. The extraordinary prolongation of the episode is especially appropriate in that this is the last detailed narrative in the central section of *A la recherche;* this is the climax of the main plot line.

In *La Fugitive*, after Albertine's departure, the rendering of time's passage changes somewhat. Episodes are not very fully developed; indications of chronology, while coherent—a year passes, ending with the narrator's springtime trip to Venice—remain subdued. However, there is much interesting thematic material of a distinctly cyclical character, as the narrator forgets Albertine. The Venice episode opens with a remarkable analogy between the Piazzetta and the church square in Combray, the description of which we quoted earlier:

> When at ten o'clock in the morning my shutters were thrown open, I saw ablaze in the sunlight, instead of the black marble into which the slates of Saint-Hilaire used to turn, the Golden Angel on the Campanile of San Marco . . . I could see nothing but it, so long as I remained in

bed, but as the whole world is merely a vast sun-dial, a single lighted segment of which enables us to tell what time it is, on the very first morning I was reminded of the shops in the Place de l'Eglise at Combray, which, on Sunday, were always on the point of shutting when I arrived for mass, while the straw in the market place smelt strongly in the already hot sunlight.

Neither Venice—so longed for in *Swann*—nor Combray has been mentioned very much in recent volumes. Likewise Gilberte and Saint-Loup come back into the narrative with the announcement of their marriage, which unites the two unjoinable ways—*côtés*—of Swann and Guermantes. The feeling of cyclical movement is further heightened when the narrator spends a short time in the summer at Balbec with the Saint-Loups and a bit later visits Gilberte at Tansonville, Swann's old estate near Combray. This second episode constitutes, furthermore, a false attempt to recapture the past: the Combray the narrator sees is nocturnal and unfamiliar. He has not yet tasted the madeleine and the cup of linden tea which will resurrect the village of his childhood. The cycle has reached a deceptive conclusion, deceptive in the sense that the narrator feels he never will be able to bring the past back to life in a work of art, and also in the sense that this is a pseudoending, a misleading cadence.

The episode of World War I, which Proust, of course, had not foreseen when he planned out his novel before 1912, serves a quite special function in *A la recherche:* as the narrator is reaching a zero point in his useless life, the world around him suddenly turns into an inferno, and our attention is once again distracted from the narrator to society in both the special and larger senses of the word. The wartime chapter in *Le temps retrouvé* contains an especially interesting mingling of time planes, which has as point of departure an evening in Paris in early 1916. The narrator had been on a visit to the capital at the outbreak of the war, but to avoid simply putting the two episodes side by side, with no tighter relationship between them than chronological sequence, the 1914 trip is told as part of the later one in order to achieve a significant connection between the two. The structure of the passage shows how skillfully Proust can base an elaborate development on a slender device: the narrator sets out to see Mme Verdurin, which permits a description of her new position and of wartime society; the unfamiliar, blacked-out look of Paris calls up memories, by contrast, of his stay there in 1914 and his talks with Saint-Loup; these thoughts bring to mind Saint-Loup's visit of the preceding day; the narrator then meets and talks lengthily with Charlus, and, finally, lost in the darkness, having given up all hope of finding the Verdurins, he stops in the brothel—taking it for a hotel—which Jupien runs for the baron, and then he returns home. A wealth of material is compactly and cohesively presented by this simple mechanism of having the narrator set out on a fruitless walk. It allows in particular the extraordinary juxtaposition of three images of Saint-Loup: his detached lack of fanaticism in 1914, his bravery and absorption in the spirit of warfare in 1916, and, finally, his furtive exit from Jupien's "hotel." By this yoking together of contrasted images Proust builds up one of his finest paradoxical portraits of a person in whom high moral and intellectual qualities are incomprehensibly mingled with vice, as is splendidly symbolized by Saint-Loup's losing his *croix de guerre* in the male brothel. Such an effect is made possible by working the three appearances of Saint-Loup into the fabric of one continuous episode, even though only one of them properly belongs to it.

Never is the narrator so reticent about himself as in the course of his sanatorium stays, before, during, and after the war. This is the personal nadir; he has ceased to exist for himself as well as for others. His return to Paris, "after many years," which opens the last section of *Le Temps retrouvé*, is accompanied by reflections on his stay at Tansonville, which revealed to him his incapacity for transmuting life into literature, and by his indifference to a vista of trees, a sight which had moved him once in Balbec. He is still making the mistake of believing in the objectivity of beauty: that it resides in a place, person, or thing. Demonstration of the contrary awaits him almost immediately when he arrives at the Guermantes' house and is ushered into the library to await a break in the concert taking place in the *grand salon*.

As he reaches the Guermantes' and waits in the library, the narrator goes through an unexpected series of experiences of involuntary memory which bring back to him life in Combray, Balbec, and Venice. They conclude and complement a number of "privileged moments" scattered throughout the novel.[2] The narrator now realizes that this form of memory will permit him to write a work of literature, which, furthermore, by its very method, will be meaningful to everyone. The reader feels the circle of *A la recherche* to have come full swing: the way in which Combray was resurrected in the first part of *Swann* is made into a general principle, and the narrator has already recreated certain essential landscapes in his mind. But there is more to Proust's novel; the lengthy scene of the reception follows, and there the narrator's

[2] Their number can be variously calculated, for their individual characteristics are quite different. For this question, as well as their role in the conclusion of the novel, see Shattuck, 36–39, 69–78.

reflections on time have nothing to do with involuntary memory—which denies and defies time—but rather spring from observation and experience. Proust recognized, alongside the ultimate truth of the imagination, a more pedestrian form of truth that comes from the intelligence; in fact, the work of art depends on the lower truths to create a setting, in the jeweler's sense, for higher revelations.

Proust's novel is the first one in French that even a careful reader cannot take in entirely at once. Its spatial qualities—the circle closed in the Guermantes' library, and so forth—have often been commented on, but perhaps the best proof of their importance lies exactly in the fact that endless details of the texture have little meaning without reference to later episodes. Nor are these details comparable to the clues or anticipatory hints common in traditional nineteenth-century plots: they are not placed in such a way as to draw attention to themselves. In sum, this elaborate design is highly reflexive rather than being constructed in the accretive, additive fashion commoner in novels.[3]

A la recherche is too vast and complex, its style too original to be placed in comparison with other developments in the evolution of fictional technique. However, Proust's use of the first person is only the most extraordinary example of it in a period when the major tendencies in French fiction were the opposite of the

3 For further discussion of problems in Proust's narrative method, see John Porter Houston, "Temporal Patterns in *A la recherche du temps perdu*," *French Studies*, XVI (January, 1962), 33–44; "Literature and Psychology: The Case of Proust," *L'Esprit Créateur*, V (Spring, 1965), 3–13; "Thought, Style, and Shape in Proust's Novel," *Southern Review*, n.s. V (October, 1969), 987–1003; and "Theme and Structure in *A la recherche du temps perdu*," *Kentucky Romance Quarterly*, XVII (1970), 209–21.

carefully worked-out, carefully narrated plot of the
nineteenth century. The neointerventionist narration, as
in *Bubu-de-Montparnasse*, *Génitrix*, or *Les Faux-Monnayeurs* was to recede in importance, as was also the deceptive first person of *Le Grand Meaulnes* or *La Symphonie
pastorale*. Both of these techniques might be considered
even more self-conscious than Flaubert's elaborate pre-
tense of impersonality; both draw attention to the con-
trived quality of fiction. It is quite likely this obtrusive
air of polish and plan which impelled a younger genera-
tion of writers toward still other first-person forms
that seemed more natural (only, of course, to appear
artificial to even later writers), less studied in use of
point of view, and finally, giving a certain air of sincerity through tone, style, and presentation of events.

Sincerity is naturally an illusion, like everything else
in fiction, but the methods by which such illusions are
obtained concern us here. Forms resembling the journal,
as well as the journal itself, become especially prominent.
Radiguet's *Le Diable au corps* (1923), for example, while
obviously meant to be written well after the events of
the story, since the narrator assumes in turn his adolescent point of view and a mature, reflective attitude, is
composed of short, detached passages, sometimes less
than a page in length, as if the episodes were being presented in a kind of living, undigested disorder. Radiguet's fondness for the maxim and an occasional hint of
the neoclassical language of psychology make clear its
filiation with confessions such as *Adolphe*, but the fitful,
sober narrative movement makes it very much a part of
the twentieth-century rediscovery of the first person.
Sometimes, as in Céline's *Voyage au bout de la nuit*
(1932), we find a very willful avoidance of structuring
events into plotlike patterns which assimilates a novel

to the journal form. In *L'Etranger* (1942), on the other hand, there is an element of thickening plot, but the tone and sentence patterns established at the beginning of the narrative disassociate it from usual notions of written language. But again, the criterion of colloquialness is not, in itself, sufficient to isolate the current of fiction we are discussing: Camus at points becomes evocative and poetic; Céline varies his original argot style with quite grand flights of rhetoric, while the narrator of *La Nausée* (1938) manages at once to be familiar and to deploy a densely metaphoric style which is almost without precedent. The first-person work of Saint-Exupéry and Bernanos offers similar resistance to easy classification. However, despite variations in technique, all these writers seem to share the feeling that the realities of certain kinds of experience cannot be rendered through the third person: the lonely, perceptive individual startled by a new direction in his inner life or increasingly aware of vast, occult forces in the world does best to speak directly to a reader he is not trying to deceive but make understand. But what perhaps most of all makes us see the relations between these novelists is the development of quite different patterns in fiction in the 1950s.[4]

The New Novelists of the mid-century, while varying in the use of specific devices, aimed characteristically at what one might call a new conception of impersonality in fiction. Someone speaks. It may be in first, second, or third person, present or past tense; in the New Novel such distinctions tend to lose their previous importance. The voice belongs to a person, of course, but he does not

[4] For characteristic techniques before and after World War II, see W. M. Frohock, *Style and Temper: Studies in French Fiction, 1925–1960* (Cambridge, Mass., 1969).

characterize himself, tell us about himself. Even when the voice says odd things and is almost consistent in his oddities, his is not a clearly definable personality. We know only what passes through his mind, and if the novel is in the third person, the narration is nothing more than the content of the consciousness of someone called by a certain name. And the speaking consciousness may melt into, or be suddenly replaced by another one. The imaginary, as well as evocations of present, past, and future, may pass through the voice's mental stream. Fragmentary dialogue may be heard. Chronology is not necessarily observed, and elements of plot, often minimal to start with, may remain unresolved, or the reality of happenings is unascertainable. This kind of technique (I have been describing, of course, an ideal New Novel made up of elements common to a number of them) produces a piece of writing which is like a seamless web: no place is left for the impure dualities of character and setting, plot and psychology, author and character, narrating voice and the people it presents to us. The New Novelists have carried the fictional illusion beyond the point where one can anatomize such abstractions. All manner of theoretical difficulties in fictional technique are solved with this ingenious narrative method, and I think it must be considered to have completely freed itself from nineteenth-century realism, certain elements of which persist even in the most sophisticated first-person novels of earlier decades. But whether or not it will give rise to a lengthy new development in the novel remains, of course, to be seen.

Index